Restaurant Design
Bethan Ryder

Published in 2004 by Laurence King Publishing Ltd
71 Great Russell Street
London WC1B 3BP
Tel: +44 20 7430 8850
Fax: +44 20 7430 8880
e-mail: enquiries@laurenceking.co.uk
www.laurenceking.co.uk

A catalogue record for this book is available from the
British Library.

ISBN: 1 85669 363 5

Printed in China

Designed by Blast, London. www.blast.co.uk
Special photography (pages 3, 5, 18, 66, 88, 116, 160):
Rob Lawson

LAURENCE KING

Restaurant Design
Bethan Ryder

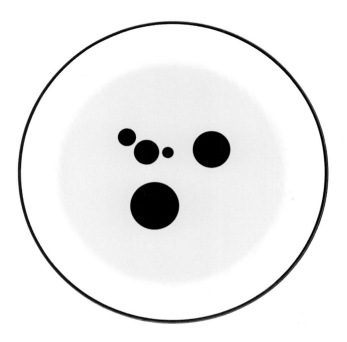

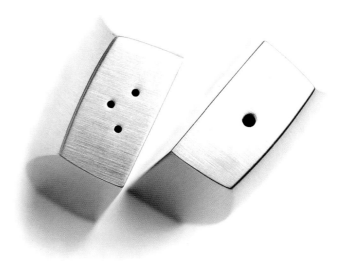

Left:
A Roman fresco uncovered
at the city of Herculaneum –
destroyed by the great Mount
Vesuvius eruption of 79AD –
depicts the fashionable Roman
ritual of reclining dining.

Restaurant, noun: A place where people pay to sit and eat meals that are cooked and served on the premises. [origin: early 19th cent. French *restaurer*, 'provide food for' (literally to 'restore to a former state')] *The New Oxford Dictionary of English*

Dining out in the developed world of the 21st century has become as much a source of entertainment as of nourishment. Restaurateurs, architects and designers are producing theatrical, themed and spectacular interiors designed to seduce, impress and amaze. Since the grand banquets of Greek and Roman times, and earlier, eating with others in public has been associated with entertainment and performing arts such as music and dance. However, the reality of a fixed public place where people go to dine for pleasure and entertainment in itself emerged more recently, in the form of the restaurant. This dining institution is specifically a mid-18th-century French invention, as first documented by gastronome Jean-Anthelme Brillat-Savarin (in *The Physiology of Taste*) in 1826; now, nearly 200 years later, the sheer number of restaurants around the world suggests that he was correct when he surmised in his treatise that the man who founded the restaurant was 'a genius endowed with profound insight into human nature'.

An article in *World Architecture* (no. 60, October 1997) estimated that there were 80,000 restaurants in Tokyo, 15,000 in New York and 10,000 in London – and rising. Proud denizens of both New York and London could legitimately boast during the late 1990s that their city was 'the restaurant capital of the world'. Certainly, the last 20 years have seen an almost unprecedented restaurant boom in most major cities and the diversity of food and establishment type is astounding. Consumer expectation has risen dramatically, compounded by modern technology and communications, which have made us internationally mobile and given us a sophisticated awareness of other cultures and foods. All of this is reflected in the rich diversity of cuisine, architecture and design on display in today's restaurants. As a consequence, with so much choice and rich experience, restaurants have become more than simply places to eat in.

As space shrinks in the cities of the developed world and citizens have less private room to call their own, they are increasingly opting to dine out in public spaces. In our 'lifestyle'-obsessed times, these public arenas are where the modern urbanite 'performs' his or her identity – where you eat and drink defines, to an extent, your social self. As journalist Nick Foulkes remarked upon the London scene in the *Evening Standard's ES* magazine (3 March 2000), 'Over the past ten years, the concept of a restaurant visit as a special event has evaporated, or at least mutated. It is no longer a matter of lunch or dinner,

it is a lifestyle choice, and restaurants have insinuated themselves into our lives at all levels: we are where we eat. Indeed, in today's confusing world of status by stealth, the fact that you can book a table at The Ivy or Le Caprice on the day you want it says far more about you than driving the latest 7 series BMW ever could.'

Restaurants have come a long way since the first examples, but what about their antecedents? Brillat-Savarin briefly documents early notions of meals: 'Meals, in the sense in which we understand the word, began with the second age of man; that is to say, as soon as he stopped living wholly on fruits.' As man became increasingly mobile these became more social gatherings, 'the weary traveller would sit down at these primitive meals, and tell what was happening in distant lands'. He discusses the eating habits of the Greeks and Romans, lying down on *lectuli*: 'These couches, which had originally been just ordinary simple benches, with a covering of skins stuffed with straw, soon received their share of luxury which invaded everything connected with banquets. They were made of the rarest of woods, encrusted with ivory, gold and sometimes precious stones; the cushions were exquisitely soft, and the rugs which covered them were decorated with magnificent embroidery.' It is interesting to note that this style of reclining dining is making a return in the 21st century, as some projects in this book attest.

As the Christian religion became dominant in the West the *lectulum* faded out, gourmandism was regarded as a sin and such louche dining was forbidden for moral reasons. Lavish banquets disappeared altogether after the fall of the Roman Empire, only to return under the rule of Charlemagne when, as Brillat-Savarin says, 'Hospitality became a chivalrous and gallant thing'. As travel increased and trade routes developed during the mid-17th century, new consumables such as coffee, tobacco and sugar were introduced to Europe, an interest in gastronomy was revived, and under Louis XIV and Louis XV banqueting and gourmandism became quite the fashion again. These developments would lead to the birth of the restaurant.

Meanwhile, across the Channel in 16th-century London, the lack of space and domestic facilities such as ovens meant that public places to eat and buy food were essential. There were always street traders, but other institutions also provided sustenance: bread ovens and cookshops sold takeaway victuals, and taverns and inns also provided basic food alongside alcohol. 'Hot nourishing meals and ready-to-eat foods were provided by inns, ale-houses and cookshops, the forerunners of modern hotels, restaurants, pubs and snack bars, and for many Londoners the Livery Company Hall was an important venue for convivial dining and corporate entertaining,' writes Hazel Forsyth in *London Eats Out: 500 Years of Capital Dining* (Philip Wilson, 1999). In terms of 'design' these places were merely functional. Taverns offering a fixed-price meal (table d'hôte) varied from a single room

to a property with multiple rooms complete with gardens, outhouses and bowling greens. In terms of design it seems that home comforts were the main inspiration; says Forsyth of the cookshops: 'some smart ones had dining rooms, often furnished with turkey-work upholstery, hangings, carpets and curtains'.

Coffee houses emerged in the late 17th century; indeed, by 1663 there were 83 in the City of London. These were male domains where political, economic and literary issues of the day would be discussed and debated by gentlemen from all walks of life. Forsyth describes their interiors: 'Most had large sash windows set high in walls lined with panels of deal adorned with "gilt frames containing an abundance of Rarieties" simply furnished with tables, stools, benches and the grander establishments with leather upholstered chairs.' Coffee houses focused on selling non-alcoholic drinks and, as a democratic alternative to the tavern, can be considered precursors to the restaurant, as Samantha Hardingham points out in 'The Design of Dining Out in London: Sit Facing In' (in *Food and Architecture*, Wiley-Academy, 2002). She explains how, due to government legislation limiting the growth of coffee houses in 1675 and the protests of women a century later, they had almost disappeared: 'Any coffee house that was political in character became a private club (and then a grand restaurant in its own right) … and others turned into chophouses or taverns.'

Before we can fully understand how the restaurant appeared in London we must return to France. Prior to being a place to eat, a *restaurant* was a restorative broth or soup, otherwise known as *bouillon*. As Edwina Ehrman explains in '18th Century' (*London Eats Out*, Philip Wilson, 1999): 'The word "restaurant" first appeared in the 16th century meaning any food which restores, but it came to be used more specifically to describe particularly reviving soup. By 1771 the definition also included "an establishment specializing in the sale of restorative foods".'

According to popular wisdom it was a certain Parisian bouillon-seller, Monsieur Boulanger, who really changed the etymology when he became involved in what Sir Terence Conran refers to as 'an amusing little dispute' (*Restaurants*, Conran Octopus, 2000). Boulanger opened his soup room in 1765, advertising his wares with a sign over the door declaring, 'Boulanger sells restoratives fit for the Gods' and 'I will restore you' (*Ego restaurabo vos*). This would not have been a problem had Boulanger not devised a new dish – sheep's feet in white wine sauce – at a time in France when the guilds ruled and only the cook-caterers, or *traiteurs*, officially had the right to serve full meals, cooked meats in sauces and *ragoûts*. When Boulanger defied these rules and presented his customers with the new dish, the *traiteurs* fought him in the courts, but the pioneering entrepreneur won, his new dish became the flavour of the day and more enterprising individuals followed in his footsteps.

Left:
Although women often ran coffee houses they were solely male domains, as this illustration from 1705 shows. Note the simple furnishings and large fire to roast the beans and keep the coffee pots warm.

Right:
A later, more luxurious coffee house is depicted in this colour etching dated 1819.

As Brillat-Savarin wrote, 'Finally the restaurant has made its appearance; a completely new and inadequately recognized institution, the effect of which is that any man with three or four *pistoles* in his purse can immediately, infallibly, and simply for the asking, procure all the pleasures of which taste is susceptible.' For a time these establishments remained a strictly French institution, as Rebecca Spang explains in *The Invention of the Restaurant* (Harvard University Press, 2000): 'Until well after the middle of the 19th century, restaurants were to remain an almost exclusively Parisian phenomenon, one rarely encountered outside the French capital. American and English travellers to Paris marvelled at its restaurants, terming them amongst the city's "most peculiar" and "most remarkable" features.' Even throughout the rest of France the restaurant was relatively unknown. 'As late as 1851, local officials in nearly two-thirds of France's provincial departments reported that their jurisdictions had no restaurants.' They did not count inns or wine shops, where people could eat; the restaurant was considered a different thing altogether: 'An aura of sophistication, novelty and mystery still clung to the terms and the space, and something very specific was meant when people talked about "restaurants".' It is precisely these establishments that are the predecessors of the projects featured in this book.

London of course soon followed Paris fashion, as Ehrman notes: 'Mr Horton, a confectioner, set up a soup room in Cornhill, which offered a fantastic dining experience in the latest French style. An engraving of about 1770 shows an elegant vaulted room hung with Venetian mirrors and stucco swags.' During the 18th century the general emphasis on pleasure changed the whole attitude to eating out in London. As the middle classes grew, social mobility was all: 'To fulfil their ambitions they spent money on fashion, leisure and entertainment. In this competitive environment where "seeing and being seen" was all-important, eating out assumed a new significance,' says Ehrman. At this stage, design, or at least comfort, became one of the advertised attractions; victuallers began to emphasize 'genteel accommodation and the novelty and fashion of the fixtures and fittings'. Certainly some effort was made in inns, too: they would often be hierarchically divided between the hall, and kept sparse and plain to accommodate the budget traveller; the parlour would be decorated with rather more bourgeois elements – china, ornaments and birdcages, and pictures and maps on the walls. Space-maximizing mirrors became popular and lighting became more considered. Taverns remained mainly male environments and steadfastly functional, as did the new chophouses, usually furnished with simple bench seating with a clock as the only adornment.

It was not until the 19th century that the restaurant truly bloomed. In post-Revolutionary France the growth of the middle classes brought with it a proliferation of restaurants, and the many comfortable, elaborate dining salons serving 'haute cuisine', once the preserve of the aristocracy, were increasingly accessible; dining out was relatively democratized. During and after the Revolution many chefs travelled to England and the New World, spreading their culinary expertise and flair for hospitality. Conran cites several individuals who were responsible for establishing classic French cuisine abroad, the most important of whom was Marie-Antoine Carême, who began as private chef to one of Napoleon's officers and went on to work for the Prince Regent (later George IV) at the Royal Pavilion, Brighton. Chefs Alexis Soyer and Auguste Escoffier trained under Carême and then took their talent and knowledge to the grand hotels and luxurious gentlemen's clubs of 19th-century London – to the Reform Club and the Savoy Hotel, respectively. Louis-Eustache Ude, former chef to Louis XVI, presided over the grand kitchens at the elite gambling club Crockfords. As this gastronomic wave gathered momentum, cookery books and restaurant guidebooks emerged, in which dining rooms were 'praised for being well lit, spacious, tastefully fitted up and clean, and criticized for poor ventilation'. Taste, whether of the palate or the eye, was beginning to matter.

There are many parallels to be drawn between the proliferation and prominence of commercial leisure spaces at the beginning of the 21st century, and those that emerged during the late 19th and early 20th century. The resurgence of cocktail culture and the fact that cafés, bars, restaurants, lounges and hotels are burgeoning suggests a *fin-de-siècle* renaissance, a cyclical repetition of that golden age a century ago. Nowhere was this more excessive than in the New World, as William Grimes in *Straight Up or On the Rocks: A Cultural History of American Drink* (Simon & Schuster, 1993) reported of the late 19th century: 'It was the age of "more is more", and not only in decoration. America took an uncomplicated attitude towards wealth and display …. The oxymoronic notion of intimate public space did not exist. Life outside the home was lived on a theatrical, heroic scale.' This was a time of millionaires, and the rich wanted to celebrate their lavish lifestyles in public, hence the need for bars, restaurants and hotels.

In London and New York the hotel was reinvented as a grand establishment offering entertainment outside the home. Women were beginning to dine in public with men – indeed, as Ehrman points out, 'Increasingly middle class demands for respectable eating places, suitable for members of both sexes, undoubtedly encouraged the growth of restaurants.' In the New World, and more specifically New York, there had also been taverns, inns and street stalls, beaneries and coffeecake salons. But the first classy stand-alone restaurant based on the French style was Delmonico's. Originally a small pastry and confectionery shop owned by the eponymous Swiss

brothers Peter and John, it grew into a grand dining room designed to entice New York's social elite. The interior was sumptuous, with ornate gilt mirrors, fancy wallpaper and luxurious patterned curtains. By 1860 there were two branches, one uptown on the corner of Broadway and one downtown, called the Citadel.

More glamorous venues followed. Murray's on Time Square was apparently known for its elaborate fantasy interiors, with each room decorated in a different exotic style. There was the legendary Waldorf-Astoria, and also Sherry's. In typical larger-than-life New York fashion these were grand emporia devoted to pleasure and entertainment, and often included tea parlours, ballrooms and private dining rooms gathered under one opulent roof. This trend has recently been revived with the likes of Sketch in London and Villa Zevaco in Casablanca. As Jayne Merkel points out, 'In the 19th and 20th centuries, grandeur in design was most often found in hotel restaurants, such as the pioneering white marble Fifth Avenue Hotel … where the dining room was lined with Corinthian columns and chandeliers hung from a colourful vaulted ceiling' ('Eating Out in New York', in *Food & Architecture*, Wiley-Academy 2002). Unfortunately none of these early hotel restaurants survives; even the seminal Delmonico's was defeated by Prohibition and closed in 1923.

In many cities the mid- to late 19th century was a time of growth. Certainly in London during the 1860s the catering industry became more commercialized. According to Ehrman, 116 companies involved in the hotel and restaurant sector were registered between 1866 and 1884. Many of these new restaurants were modelled on Continental establishments and often run by Frenchmen or Swiss-Italians. Indeed, when it came to design and fine dining the ornate, grandiose French look predominated as the template for some time. In London, for example, Ehrman says of café-restaurants: 'They were decorated in the Continental style with plate glass mirrors, red plush and lavish gilding, but the cuisine was usually English or Anglo-French.' Simpson's on the Strand opened in 1848, 'a light and spacious dining room furnished with tables as well as boxes. Its retention of boxes shows it to have been a transitional layout, but it had more of the ambience of a restaurant or club dining room than a chophouse.'

According to Terence Conran huge restaurant complexes such as Romanov's, the Café Royal (opened 1865) and the Trocadero (opened 1896) 'were places of immense luxury. Lavishly decorated, with a wealth of marble and mirror, plush and gilt, potted palms and accompanying orchestras – and huge – the Café Royal fed 600 a night.' Ehrman describes the gloriously Byzantine Criterion Restaurant and Theatre, designed by Thomas Verity, which opened in 1874: 'Its spacious and varied accommodation, opulent interiors and comfortable carpeted dining areas with flowers on the tables set the

Left:
The lavish gilt and red velvet interior of the Grill Room at London's Café Royal, which is still in use today for private functions, was modelled on the elaborate interiors of Paris restaurants. Actor and agent Sir Herbert Tree once commented, 'If you want to see English people at their most English, go to the Café Royal where they are trying their hardest to be French.'

Right:
London's Criterion restaurant is considered by some to be Thomas Verity's finest work. Built on the site of the 17th-century White Bear Inn, it comprised a basement theatre, the Marble Hall and Long Bar on the ground floor, dining rooms on the first and second floors and a ballroom on the top floor. Owner Marco Pierre White commissioned designer David Collins to restore it to its former gilded glory in the late 1990s.

Bottom:
Diners at the exquisite Train Bleu are enchanted and entertained by 41 richly coloured frescos illustrating the cities that passengers passed through en route from Paris to Lyon and the south of France.

benchmark for future developments'. These spectacular interiors were no doubt modelled on the French and Viennese Belle-Epoque style, a rich decorative aesthetic that exudes prosperity and *joie de vivre*. This elaborate look had quite a legacy in France. Le Grand Véfour, originally opened in 1784, is considered *the* great original French restaurant. The grand decor of mirrored walls, gilded furnishings and classical figures painted onto plaster columns set the tone for many smart Parisian restaurants, for example Le Train Bleu in the Gare de Lyon, built for the 1900 Exposition Universelle.

Grand hotels were often host to some of the finest restaurants. London followed Paris and New York's example in this area, and from the late 1860s many London hotels had grill rooms following the US tradition. The Savoy, designed by Richard D'Oyly Carte and opened in 1889, was created specifically to attract American guests; it was here that César Ritz and Auguste Escoffier made their reputations.

During the 20th century these trends continued to evolve and dining out became far more democratized, although until the 1960s there was little on offer between the very basic dining experience and the elaborate, grand affair. The 'bright young things' era between the wars led to the creation of 'dance restaurants', cabarets and nightclubs, and the luxurious speakeasies of Prohibition America. In London restaurants of the 1930s a lighter design style became favoured after the chef Marcel

Boulestin opened his Covent Garden restaurant in 1927, with panels painted by Jean Labourer and fabric designed by Raoul Dufy. 'Boulestin's set a tone of light, modern chic that others were to follow in preference to the heavy and rich Belle Epoque styles that characterized the older luxury restaurants,' reports Kathy Ross in '20th Century' (in *London Eats Out*).

After World War II inexpensive, functional dining spaces emerged and proliferated to cater for more basic eating experiences. These ranged from bistros, brasseries and cafés in France to automats and diners in New York, and bistros, cafés and fast-food chains in London. Travel became widely available, leading to more sophisticated tastes, and immigration also led to a growth in the diversity of foods on offer in the cities of the developed world. Design was important, as it was necessary for people to be able to identify the type of establishment and food on offer. In London, at least with regard to imitations of the American fast-food chains during the 1950s and 1960s, design was, says Kathy Ross, a 'powerful tool in turning restaurants into amusing, attractive places. *Design* magazine (February 1966) approved the trend, if not the results: 'The point is that the values now going into the restaurants interiors are design values, however crudely expressed.' A good example of how design was used to sell a mid-market brand is the UK chain Pizza Express: Peter Boizot opened the first Continental-style restaurant in London in 1965, its 'crisp, stylish, white-tiled look' created specifically to appeal to more discerning tastes.

Far left:
Mirabelle, first popular during the 1950s and 1960s, was purchased by Marco Pierre White in 1998 and refurbished by architect and designer David Collins.

Centre:
In 2000 architects Diller + Scofidio renovated the legendary basement brasserie designed by Philip Johnson in the Mies van der Rohe Seagram tower in New York. Damaged by fire in 1995, the new incarnation is slightly retro with classic 1950s chairs, but also futuristic with its use of modern materials and technology.

Right:
Quaglino's – originally a 1930s ballroom – was transformed in the early 1990s by designers Terence Conran, Linzi Coppick and Keith Hobbs into a glamorous mega-dining room.

Jump to the 21st century and the richness of the restaurant scene is the result of all this, but also, and even more directly, of the affluence of the late 1980s and 1990s in such cities as New York, London and Hong Kong. Entrepreneurs seized the golden opportunity to accommodate the new wealth, providing places for those working in the finance and media industries to wine and dine in style, and offering a choice to which diners became accustomed in the final twenty years of the 20th century. Restaurateurs such as Terence Conran in London and the Baums in New York paved the way. Conran's power-dining mega-restaurants such as Quaglino's and Mezzo harked back to the grand restaurants of the 1920s and early 1930s. Certainly Conran laid the foundations for the restaurant revolution in London; entrepreneurs such as Chris Bodker, Alan Yau and Oliver Peyton soon followed with Avenue and Circus, the now international noodle chain Wagamama, and the Atlantic Bar & Grill, respectively. These men recognized the importance of design and commissioned architects to create their interiors.

More recently we have seen the emergence of chef-patrons such as Marco Pierre White and Gordon Ramsay in the UK; this has also become an international phenomenon, with super-chefs such as Alain Ducasse, Jean-Georges Vongerichten and Nobuyuki Matsuhisa opening outposts around the world. In the same way that these men have become global chefs, so too have certain designers gone global: Philippe Starck, Patrick Jouin, David Rockwell, Jordan Mozer, Karim Rashid, Christian Liagre and David Collins are all jet-setting designers creating restaurant interiors around the world. Recently there has been a revamping of the old restaurant classics. In the old hotels restaurants have been brought back to life – for example the Plaza Athénée in Paris (by chef Alain Ducasse and his designer Patrick Jouin) and Claridges in London (by chef Gordon Ramsay). In Sydney this revival of old classics can be seen at Icebergs Beach Club (see page 102), and in New York at the Seagram Brasserie. Alternatively, old banks, warehouses and disused properties are being turned over to dining. Gentrification and regeneration usually begins with leisure developments; restaurants and bars – projects such as Les Trois Garçons in London (see page 178) and Centrale in Beirut (see page 122) are testament to this.

Every city has its own personal gastronomic history and there is not the room to expand on this here. Although each city has its own character – whether because the typical plot of a New York restaurant is long and narrow, or because Sydney is a city that's all about the view – the high-style 'designer' restaurants are making their mark around the globe.

Today restaurants can look like anything from a bedroom to a spaceship, from a Buddhist temple to a souk. Providing there's somewhere to rest a plate, when it comes to inspiration the world is the restaurant designer's oyster. This book seeks to introduce the reader to the most inspirational, unusual and unique restaurant spaces from around the world, places built to seduce diners and fire the imagination – high-style destination dining rooms. Not every design facilitates a calm dining experience: a spectrum of moods is offered by the restaurants featured here, from romantic to psychedelic, from buzzing to subdued, from the sublime to the downright crazy. Not all will be to everyone's taste but, like postcards or snapshots of an unknown territory, each has something to offer the architect, designer or restaurant enthusiast.

Rather than focus on types of eating establishment – hotel restaurant, canteen, fast-food outlet, and so on – this book is divided into five chapters, each based on a loosely defined category of design style: Global, Retro-Pop, Modern Classic, High Concept and New Baroque. These are not rigid definitions (in fact several projects could fall into more than one category): they are merely an attempt to summarize some of the major trends in restaurant design in the early years of the 21st century, a kind of zeitgeist shorthand that communicates the popular themes and preoccupations of the day.

Global

This section explores restaurants whose design is either inspired by or incorporates other cultures and countries. Of the five chapters in this book it is the design of these projects that is most closely linked to the food served there. In cities such as Paris, London, New York and Sydney both North African and Asian food and culture have become extremely popular. The sheer size of this chapter suggests that travel remains a major source of inspiration in terms of food and design: the restaurants included here demonstrate how restaurant design, like food, has become a melting-pot of global styles. Just as cuisine has evolved into new hybrids, such as Pan-Asian or Pacific-Rim, so the design of many of these restaurants, for example Nirvana (see page 44) and Ginto (see page 28), suggests that there is no longer a 'pure' theme but rather often a collage of styles. Pioneering entrepreneurs introducing such concepts include Mourad Mazouz, whose North African-inspired Momo's opened in London in 1997, inspiring a wave of North African-styled restaurants. In New York Keith McNally recreated the French brasserie in the form of Balthazar – something distinctly less novel in Europe – and a host of French- and Belgian-themed restaurants, such as Markt, followed. These are proof of our fascination with different cultures: not only do people in the West, it seems, love Asian food and aesthetics – for example Tao (see page 32) or Hakkasan (see page 38) – but likewise restaurants in Tokyo and Hong Kong, such as WasabiSabi (see page 52), are adopting Western aesthetics. Architects and designers often use materials integral to the culture or country they are seeking to emulate, or apply an evocative colour scheme or integrate artworks, icons or deities in order to create their interiors.

Retro-Pop

This section reflects the nostalgic, *fin-de-siècle* trend in design that seeks to recreate the pop optimism of the 1960s and 1970s. Forerunners of this tradition include the Observation Deck restaurant at Los Angeles Airport, the Orbit bar and Summit restaurant in Harry Seidler's Australia Square tower in Sydney and Mash in Manchester (now closed) by Marc Newson. Designers producing these 'retro-futuro' spaces often employ and experiment with unusual modern materials to form fun, other-worldly interiors. The 'atomic age' is their inspiration, a time of consumer prosperity in the West when the space race led to creative movements such as Pop Art and films such as Kubrick's *2001: A Space Odyssey* (1968), and influenced designers such as Eero Aarnio and Verner Panton to create glossy, futuristic furniture and interiors. Some of the restaurants in this section, for example Pod (see page 70), seem destined for outer space. White is often the interior colour of choice; however, using new technology architects and designers are installing colour-changing lighting to drench spaces in a plethora of pastel shades – for example at Pearl (see page 78) – making them even more evocative of the optimistic candy colours of the 1960s. Vintage furniture pieces fabricated from moulded plastics and fibreglass, and materials such as epoxy resin and vinyl, combine to generate surreal environments. Some projects in this section, such as Jones (see page 68) and Rumi (see page 76), do not chase the hyper-real but nonetheless contain elements that hark back to a golden and comfortable past.

Right:
Cross-pollination keeps the restaurant industry thriving; Keith McNally's Balthazar was inspired by the simple French brasserie, something common in Europe but novel and different in New York.

Far right:
Progressive UK restaurateur Oliver Peyton commissioned Marc Newson to create the funky retro Mash restaurant brewery in Manchester (now closed). The sequel in London opened in the late 1990s, designed by architect Andy Martin, and remains successful.

Modern Classic

This chapter includes projects that could loosely be described as simple, clean spaces that do not rely on tricks, themes or grand gestures. Restaurants in this category range from minimal spaces where elements are pared down and decoration is sparse, to places where architects/designers have relied purely on classic, natural materials, such as timber or stone, to provide the adornment. The term 'classic' is not intended to conjure up the notion of a longstanding establishment (although I believe some of the projects featured will endure), but refers more to the simple materials used and the 'classic' definition of restaurant as a room with tables and chairs for dining. These projects do not stray far from their function: some, such as Locanda Locatelli (see page 98), are more luxurious, while others, such as Oggi (see page 108), are starker in their simplicity. A few of the projects here, such as Lupino (see page 94) and Coconut Groove (see page 90), are multi-purpose casual venues, open all day, by contrast with other more expensive, exclusive establishments, such as Icebergs, that cater specifically to lunch and dinner. In offering a broad view of restaurants today it is important to include projects from several European countries; this chapter has the highest proportion of projects from Spain and Germany, where less, it seems, is often considered more ….

High Concept

Restaurants in this category display truly outré design. These are places with eclectic, bizarre interiors – dining wonderlands. With these projects designers and restaurateurs have really let their imaginations run wild. Some are designed around a central concept, such as the silver clouds at Georges (see page 126), or the sculptural wave wall at Opium (see page 120), others are simply unique interiors. Predecessors to those featured here include Fabio Novembre's Shu in Milan – featuring giant golden forearms supporting the restaurant roof – and Philippe Starck's Asia de Cuba at the Mondrian, Los Angeles, with its enormous flowerpots on the terrace. Adam Tihany's Aureole in Mandalay Bay, Las Vegas, uses as its centrepiece an enormous glass-and-steel wine tower. This section encompasses a diverse range of projects, from Bernard Khoury's unusual reclamation of war-torn properties in Beirut (see pages 122 and 132) to Jordan Mozer's creation of a football club-inspired tavern in Hamburg. Some of the designs are closely related to either the restaurateur's concept or the chef's food, but they are often more intrinsically tied to the location (such as Khoury's two restaurants, Georges at the Pompidou, or Opium in Sydney). These are, without exception, incredibly innovative interiors.

Below:
The ultimate 'power dining' Pool Room designed in 1959 by Philip Johnson in the Mies van der Rohe Seagram Tower may be a modern classic, but it also contains elements of High Concept with its centrepiece of rippling pool and trees.

Top right:
Starck's 'high concept' oversized terracotta pots and arbour frame the alfresco dining at Asia de Cuba on the leafy roof terrace of the Mondrian hotel.

Bottom right:
Starck continued the dramatic theme with Madrid's Theatriz, which occupies a space that was once a theatre.

New Baroque

The shortest chapter, but certainly worth documenting, is devoted to the New Baroque style of restaurant design. Philippe Starck, who designed Bon in Paris (see page 158), is possibly the godfather of this eclectic, quirky vision, a style epitomized by Theatriz in Madrid and Felix in Hong Kong. A maximalist backlash to all things minimal and sleek, this approach mixes elaborate, antique or ornate furniture and decoration with avant-garde objects, modern pieces and sometimes also modern technology – all in a self-referential, tongue-in-cheek way. Often this is a style executed in response to an existing building: Les Trois Garçons inhabits a listed Victorian pub, for example, while the Plaza Athénée (see page 184) is an old Parisian hotel and Sketch occupies a Georgian town house (see page 168). Silver and gilt sit with modern materials such as fibreglass and moulded plastic, but a sense of old-fashioned grandeur always permeates. Although very diverse all of the examples have a decadent flourish here, a sumptuous swath of silk or velvet there, which sends them into the whimsical sphere of New Baroque.

Right:
Tihany's Aureole ignited a trend for impressive wine displays. Wines are retrieved from this 13 metre (42 foot) tall glass tower by waiters who attach themselves to harnesses in an entertaining feat of acrobatics.

Global

Deep spice colours of ochre, persimmon, purple and blue applied to rubbed plaster give **Tangerine** its earthy North African flavour

Left:
The 80-cover, 'free-floating' dining platform is enclosed by timber screens, fretwork and drapes. Access routes are lit by authentic Moroccan lanterns.

Plan:
The 700 square metre (7,500 square foot) space occupies the basement and ground floor of an office building.

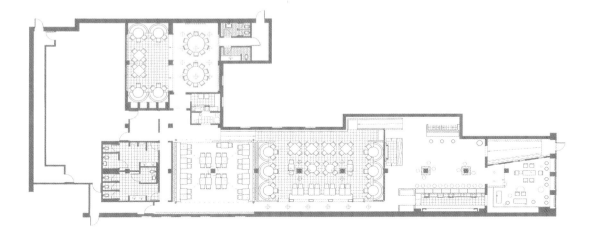

Tangerine, Philadelphia, USA
January 2000
David Schefer Design

When it comes to restaurant trends of the millennium, restaurateurs, chefs and designers are revisiting 1960s fashions thirty years on and looking to North Africa for gastronomic and visual inspiration. Morocco especially has attracted designers who recognize that its warm, earthy colours, delicate lighting and rich textures and patterns make for cosy, magical and exotic interiors. Today no (developed world) city is worth its cosmopolitan status without a restaurant, bar or club bearing souk or kasbah allusions. Prolific restaurant producer Stephen Starr commissioned New York-based designers David and Eve-Lynn Schefer to bring the modern Moroccan dining experience to Philadelphia by creating the interior for his French-inspired Moroccan restaurant in the Old City area.

Tangerine joins several other Starr-owned restaurants in this downtown district, which has developed into a popular destination frequented by urban professionals and residents of the surrounding suburbs. 'The owner requested a warm, modern and dramatic setting in which to serve an ambitious Moroccan influenced menu,' explains David Schefer. 'Since the menu was not traditional fare, he wanted an environment that made reference to Morocco without being overtly literal.' David Schefer Design have created an intriguing restaurant

interior, as they describe: 'it's an intricately layered space inspired by Moroccan fretwork and divided into a series of intimate dining experiences, punctuated by dramatic lighting, rich materials and hundreds of flickering candles.'

Diners enter the L-shaped restaurant via a candle-lined ramp leading into the reception and bar area. The French-Moroccan fusion food is signalled by three clocks above the reception desk: 'The sand-blasted faces reveal a ghostly impression of the time in Philadelphia, France and Tangiers,' says Eve-Lynn Schefer. A high-backed bench on the right artfully conceals the cloakroom. The long stainless steel bar features a glass and patterned metal top and glows with changing coloured lighting.

To the front of the restaurant, leading off from the reception/bar, is a sunken lounge furnished with low, distressed leather chairs, scatter cushions and authentic Moroccan tables and pouffes. Lighting in this room comes from a variety of sources: windows afford natural daylight, tables are candlelit, the ceiling is decorated with uplit plaster domes emitting a blue light and single candles are suspended from the larger apertures. Timber boxes with patterned wood fronts punctuate the dividing wall between the lounge and entrance corridor. Bedecked with candles, these provide eye-catching illuminated glimpses between the entrance and lounge.

The 250-cover restaurant is divided into several more intimate spaces. 'Although each area is distinct in design and feel,' says Eve-Lynn Schefer, 'they remain connected to adjacent areas through the use of screens inspired by Moroccan fretwork and veils.' The main dining area, accessible via a ramp next to the reception desk, occupies a slightly raised platform. A full-height, patterned timber screen separates this 80-cover dining area from the bar and the corridor running to the rear of the restaurant.

This space is furnished with a mosaic wood-tile floor and was 'conceived as a free-floating stage set'. To create this ephemeral, floating sensation the dining platform remains isolated from the side walls, screens and support columns, and light has been used to fill the gaps with dramatic effect. David Schefer explains: 'The lighting scheme throughout Tangerine was devised to create a dense atmospheric setting and enhance the various architectural elements; in this area lighting emanates from the gaps, creating the impression of a floating surface.' But the ultimate scene-stealer here is the ochre plaster wall, alive with candlelit Moroccan-inspired niches that send out a warm, gentle radiance.

Directly behind this dining platform is a smaller, more secluded dining area. Richly patterned surfaces engender an opulent ambience: walls are replaced with ornate velvet draperies, a patchwork of authentic Moroccan rugs lines the floor and metal lanterns cast starry, dappled light across the room. To the right of this area a large plaster arch opens out into the private dining room, decorated by starry lanterns and candlelit wall niches.

David Schefer Design attained their brief through an intelligent application of light and colour. Dark stained wood and the saturated, deep spice colours of ochre, persimmon, purple and blue applied to rubbed plaster conspire to give Tangerine its earthy, North African flavour. The rich combination of concealed coloured lighting, backlit screens, candles and perforated metal lanterns brings the scheme to life and bestows an enchanting, almost mystical ambience.

Above:
The sunken lounge at the front, furnished with genuine Moroccan pieces.

Left:
Tangerine offers secluded dining at tables surrounded by richly patterned velvet drapes.

Right:
Starry lanterns and candlelit wall niches give this small dining room an 'Arabian Nights' flavour.

Dos Caminos is a novel departure from your average Tex-Mex cantina

Opposite:
Cruciform and other geometric apertures provide glimpses of the service routes, kitchen and embossed tin wall behind.

Right:
The constellation of chunky, hand-carved lanterns casts starry shapes across the walls.

Far right:
Lattice metalwork screens are backlit to create a dramatic effect.

Plan:
The L-shaped space has a tequila bar at the front to entice patrons into the dining room behind. The kitchen and toilets are tucked in at the rear.

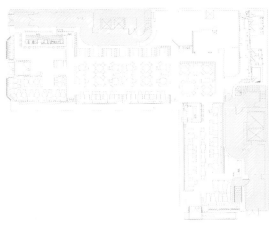

Dos Caminos, New York, USA
October 2002
Yabu Pushelberg

Toronto-based design duo George Yabu and Glenn Pushelberg describe Manhattan's Dos Caminos (two roads) restaurant as 'Chic Mexican': it's certainly a novel departure from your average Tex-Mex cantina. The pair established their practice in 1980 and now boast a 65-strong team, a Toronto HQ and New York offices and an award-winning portfolio ranging from hotels, resorts and spas to theatres, stores and restaurants. Prolific Manhattan restaurateur Stephen Hanson of the 'BR Guest' empire commissioned the pair to renovate the existing Globe Restaurant (situated on Park Avenue South) and transform it into a hip, destination Mexican restaurant. They responded by producing a 'modern interpretation of Mexican with a rustic elegant quality'.

Although it's hard to slap a label on a Yabu Pushelberg signature style, their crafted interiors display a keen exploration of textures and materials. They create to experiment and innovate, as Pushelberg says: 'We're not interested in spending 10 years refining the perfect white box, we'd rather look at a material like resin and use it 16 different ways' (New York Times, 10 October 2002). At Dos Caminos the inherited multi-hued terrazzo floor and rich, autumnal colour scheme of burnt ochres, amber and chocolate exude earthy warmth. Tin and timber have been utilized and artfully adapted to bestow a folksy, primitive character upon the interior.

According to the New York Times, Yabu Pushelberg 'like using centrepieces with obscure provenance'. Dos Caminos is no exception, with its central constellation of thirty chunky, hand-carved log lanterns. Glowing like iconic timber pumpkins, they form the twinkling core of the main dining room, which extends beyond the tequila bar at the front of the restaurant. Elsewhere, matching perforated tin pendant lights and sconces dapple the amber walls with a glitterball, alfresco fiesta effect. The theatrical lighting continues in the secluded dining room at the rear, where backlit lattice metalwork screens lend a textured luminescence.

The L-shaped space seats 275 diners, on orange banquettes and dark timber and wicker Italian chairs. Tall, gessoed metal screens, featuring quirky, Aztec-inspired symbols such as cacti, snakes and lizards, separate booths lining one side. Thick wooden tables with simple tulip bases complete the natural, hand-hewn look. At the rear of the main room a decorative wall punctuated by geometric cruciform and square apertures conceals the service routes whilst providing intriguing glimpses of the open kitchen behind. It also reveals the silver back wall lined with stamped tin sheets, embossed to appear like timber bricks complete with a wood-grain texture. This material has been used in the bar area and to frame mirrors, such as the angled, space-enhancing landscape mirror in the main dining room.

Dos Caminos has proved so popular that a sequel, Dos Caminos SoHo, opened in Spring 2003. The 'two roads' look is set to run and run.

Left:
Veiled lighting imbues the
74-seater dining room with
a softer ambience.

The cool, clean monochrome palette of Tokyo's Ginto embodies Yasumichi Morita's belief that the food should always take centre stage

Ginto, Tokyo, Japan
April 2002
Glamorous

The cool, clean monochrome palette of Tokyo's Ginto embodies designer Yasumichi Morita's belief that when it comes to restaurant design, the food should always take centre stage. Ginto translates as 'Silver Rabbit', a name that refers to the French influences of the Western-inspired fusion food. The restaurant occupies the fourth floor of a building close to Ikebukoro train station, which transports commuters between their city offices and the surrounding suburbs. Although the owner simply asked for a 'stylish restaurant', he was no doubt aware of Morita's innovative reputation. Morita is omething of a design visionary, and his Glamorous studio is responsible for many distinctive Japanese restaurant interiors.

Ginto offers dining on a large scale. Although it seats 240 people, the space is divided into several areas with varying atmospheres. Patrons arrive by elevator and approach Ginto via a black, granite-paved corridor illuminated by a frosted mirror wall hung with chrome-plated chain-balls. Revolving projectors installed in the ceiling cast wavy, flame-like lighting across the silver-white wall. The simple silver/monochrome theme continues inside. The black granite floor runs throughout the main dining space, juxtaposed with white, custom-made vinyl leather and mirror-finished stainless steel furniture. Seating in the informal main dining area is organized around the open kitchen. Single diners are accommodated at a white dupon corian counter looking on to the kitchen, which is shielded only by a veil of silver chain-beading. A long communal table running parallel to the kitchen seats couples and foursomes and towards the rear, six semicircular booths enclosed by glinting chain-bead curtains seat larger groups. Lighting maestro Morita tailor-made the frosted cylindrical acrylic pipe lamps: positioned between each booth, they appear like pure shafts or pillars of light.

Left:
Glass partitions and silver beads that hang from the ceiling generate a sense of intimacy without compromising the communal table atmosphere.

Plan:
The 620 square metre (6,674 square foot) restaurant is divided into several smaller dining sections.

To the left of the main space is a smaller private dining room, which seats 74 diners. White lace drapes, concealed pendant lights radiating a soft glow and the beige terrazzo floor generate a softer, romantic ambience. Bespoke monochrome furniture is arranged around white tables, and frosted acrylic pipe lamps, fixed to the centre of the glass-topped master table for 20, illuminate Yumi Tohyama's calligraphy on plastic laminate.

Ginto is full of Yin Yang contrasts: this gentle environment is a stark contrast to the dark, moody booths tucked behind the white circular ones. Here, seven sombre compartments with black tables (made from melamine resin-overlaid board) are separated by fourfold wire mesh and lit only by moon-like globe lamps above and an eerie runway light-strip sunk into the aisle. Opposite these are several 16-cover dining chambers divided by black fourfold wire mesh and decorated by Tohyama's calligraphy panels. Elsewhere, darkness and shadow become light: in the adjoining ten-cover dining salons Morita has created textured walls like drifting snow by applying urethane foam (fireproofing material), then adding protective layers of paint and glass.

Although elements of Ginto, such as Tohyama's artwork, are intrinsically Japanese, it is not heavily themed. Morita says: 'We weren't aiming for a Japanese style. What we wanted was a design that's groundbreaking without being futuristic – an interior that reflects the eating habits of unpredictable urban dwellers' (*Frame*, no. 29, November/December 2002). If anything, Ginto, with its minimal palette of materials, is a remarkable example of the pure theatricality that can be achieved through the manipulation of light and dark and the stark drama of black and white – the Yin and the Yang.

Left:
Half a dozen white booths accommodate diners, who sit on white, leather-upholstered sofas at dupon corian tables.

Opposite:
Smaller dining chambers at the rear of Ginto are screened off from access routes and separated from each other by a black fourfold wire mesh.

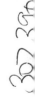

Tao's soaring, high-vaulted ceiling and towering Buddha denote grandeur on an 'awesome' Big Apple scale

Left:
Tao's colossal Buddha
appears to float effortlessly
above an infinity pool.

Right:
A view from the mezzanine
level showing the Buddha
altarpiece and hand-painted
parchment canopies above.

Tao, New York, USA
October 2000
Thomas Schoos Design Inc.

Paris's Buddha Bar may have ignited the trend
for the sacred prophet appearing somewhere in a city near
you, but for sheer spectacle New York City's Tao, Asian
bistro restaurant and bar, far outshines them all. Located
in Manhattan's midtown theatre district, the property dates
back to the mid-19th century, when it was the Vanderbilt
family's stable. Before its most recent $3.2-million majestic
reincarnation, it had been the Plaza movie theatre since the
1950s. New York restaurateur Marc Packer commissioned
Los Angeles-based design consultancy Thomas Schoos
Design to create a 'unique interior with a sanctuary feel'.
The result is this cavernous temple to all things Asian.

The drama of Tao unfolds before your eyes.
Patrons enter from the street through carved antique
Chinese doors into the small, dusky lobby decorated by a
Buddha fountain set into a stacked ledger stone setting.
To the left is the cloakroom and on the right the reception,
which leads through to the ground floor lounge bar. Natural
materials and themes, such as the slate stone used for the

bar counter, the wood used for the tables and the earthy
tones of the green and blue upholstery, are enriched by a
low, gold ceiling burnished by candlelight and red silk
lighting fixtures. Moving from this moodily lit den into the
dining area, the contrast in terms of volume of space is
quite breathtaking.

Tao's soaring 13 metre (42 foot) high vaulted
ceiling denotes grandeur on a dazzling Big Apple scale.
Even more impressive is the towering altarpiece, a 5 metre
(16 foot) Buddha monolith, positioned so that it appears to
effortlessly float above a 1.2 metre (4 foot) high infinity pool.
As Schoos says, 'I wanted it to embody the larger than life
aesthetics of Manhattan, whilst serving as a touchstone for
the Asian philosophies inherent in Tao.' Natural and artificial
light conspire to enhance the shrine-like quality of Tao and
bring the statue to life. Flickering candlelight from giant
candles arranged in wall niches behind it throws the icon
into relief, while uplighting illuminates the serenity of
Buddha's face and bathes the figure in coloured lighting
that changes from warm orange to a calming blue. This is
contrasted with the raw urban essence of the space,
emphasized by uplighting and iron sconces which give
prominence to the warmth of the brick and construction
scars from its past.

Left:
Red silk light fixtures and a
golden ceiling lend the dark
lounge bar a warm glow.

Right:
Semi-circular banquettes
seat groups of diners along
one side of the ground-floor
dining room.

Below right:
Formerly the projection room,
the Sky Box now plays host to
private dining and VIP guests.

The ground floor dining room seats 200 diners
on semicircular banquettes and chairs; the kitchen is in the
basement. Custom-designed Egyptian alabaster cylinders,
each containing a votive candle, emit a gently diffused light
from the centre of each ebonized oak table. At Buddha's
feet a hollow, glass-topped stone bath-table reveals petals
floating on water below. A further 150 diners are
accommodated on the mezzanine level, and above that in
the 'Sky Box', a private dining room with a grand view,
housed in what was once the cinema projection booth.

On the mezzanine level there is a sushi bar and
a second, semicircular cocktail bar providing barflies with
the perfect view of Buddha's face. Artefacts procured from
China, Japan and Thailand emphasize the Eastern
aesthetic, as does a backlit screen featuring photographic
portraits of Asian people. Completing the theme are huge
iron 'beehive' lanterns and a parchment canopy fabricated
from three large, hand-painted panels suspended from the
ceiling and bearing ancient Japanese poems. Tao gives
good karma but in a decidedly upfront, New York way.

Nomads offers guests a trip
into another world, to experience the exoticism
of Arabian Nights

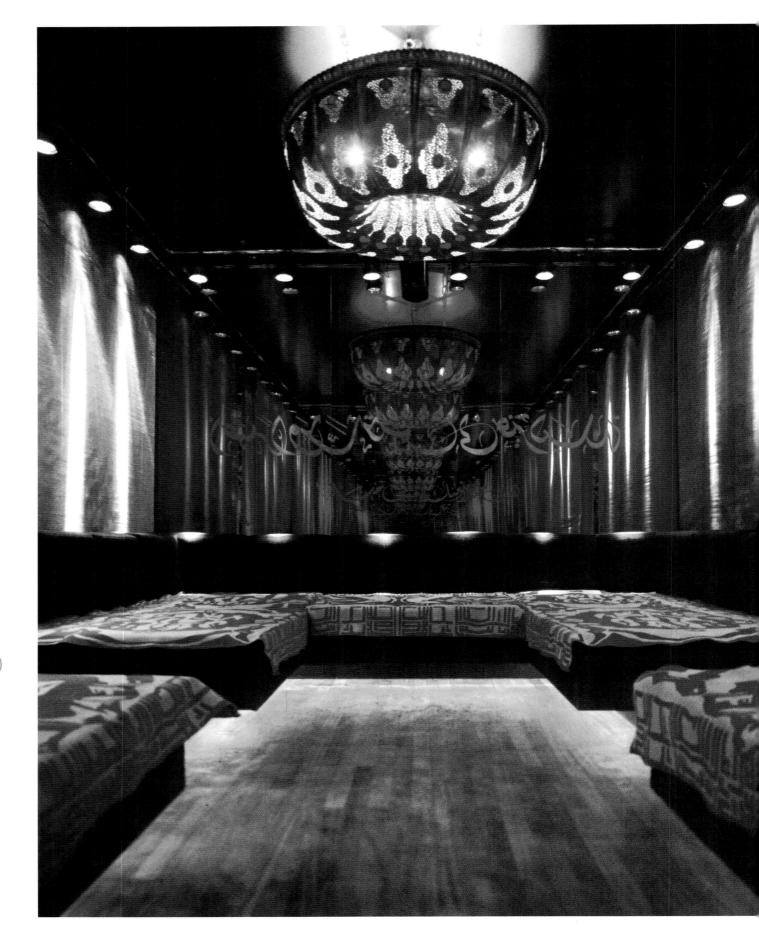

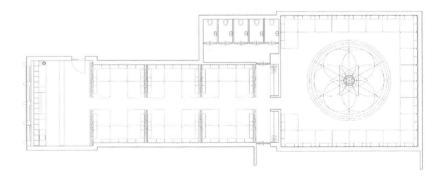

Opposite:
Dinner is served at the same
time to everyone in the dining
booths and arrives on brass
tables and trays.

Above:
The contrasting bar lobby,
where it's 'constantly daylight'
and where guests can leave
their sorrows behind.

Plan and section:
The bar lobby leads through
to the dining area, which
opens out into the 'temple' at
the rear. Here, guests dance
beneath a star-filled canopy.

Nomads, Amsterdam, The Netherlands
June 2001
Concrete Architectural Associates

Concrete are rapidly establishing themselves
as *the* mavericks of escapist interiors. Their restaurant-
nightclub concept, Nomads, offers guests a trip into
another world, to experience the exoticism of Arabian
Nights. Yet it's just on their doorstep, on the first floor of
their studio building in Amsterdam. Concrete's Rob
Wagemans explains: 'There are a lot of Arabian people in
Holland and there is a whole new generation who were
born here. So they are Dutch but have Arabian insight
because their parents pass on their culture. We wanted to
create a restaurant that has the same feeling, a hybrid of
the rich culture of Arabia but made from innovative Western
materials – the best of both worlds.' The East meets West
theme extends to the food and music too.

Beyond huge steel entrance doors, the
rectilinear space has been organized into three distinct
zones: a bar lobby, the dining area divided into six niches
and a temple at the rear, which is used for dining but
each evening evolves into a club. The bar operates as a
transitional space where patrons arrive and start to 'leave
their sorrows behind'. 'This is the only place where you
can see some daylight and where we've used cold colours
like green and blue; the rest of the interior is completely
red and gold,' says Wageman. By day, natural light filters
through the transparent coloured-glass display boxes of
the back bar; by night, artificial lights maintain the same
effect: 'It's constantly daylight so that guest lose all
sense of time.'

Eastern opulence reigns in the restaurant.
Ornate, handcrafted Moroccan 'light bowls' are the
centrepieces of each dining compartment; golden brass
mesh partitions separate booths without compromising the
communal atmosphere. Concrete reclaimed and reinvented
these mesh components, which are more commonly
(though usually steel) parts of bed frames. Each booth
accommodates a dozen diners, who recline across beds
draped in Egyptian-style kelims designed by Dutch artist
Barbara Broekman. Spotlights produce shafts and pools of
light throughout, enhancing the warm red and gold hues,

reflected and intensified by red mirrors lining the walls and
bearing the inscription of a poem in Arabic. Written by the
highly respected poet Majnoun around 800AD, it was
carefully selected: 'We chose the poem because it's about
love and having a good time.'

By the end of the night Nomad's hedonists
flock to the temple in pursuit of that good time. 'It's like an
orgy in there, everyone lying together sipping cocktails,'
says Wagemans. Guests dance beneath a glittering
canopy, stepping across stars that decorate traditional
Moroccan floor tiles. The spotlit carousel dome is
fabricated from a material otherwise found at fairgrounds:
'It's polyester; bumper cars are made from the same
substance so it's plastic but it looks like glamorous sparkly
metal.' Rock the kasbah.

A temple of Oriental chic, Hakkasan is tucked in down a back alley in London's West End

Opposite:
Hakkasan's bar on the side, Ling Ling, is furnished with bespoke embroidered leather sofas and chairs.

Above left:
Bottles on the back bar are dramatically backlit to create strong silhouettes against the rough-textured slate tiles.

Above right:
The dragon makes a spectacular return, appearing on the gold and red embroidered backs of the leather lounge-bar chairs.

Hakkasan, London, UK
May 2001
Christian Liaigre

When it comes to creating new dining concepts Hong Kong-born, London-based restaurateur Alan Yau certainly seems to have the Midas touch. Whether offering Asian food at high street prices or at the expensive, haute cuisine level, his restaurants thrive. During the 1990s he developed the minimalist blonde 'communal' diner Wagamama in London with architects John Pawson and David Chipperfield, sold the concept in 1997 and moved on to sign up chic French designer Christian Liaigre to create the accessible Thai restaurant Busaba Eathai – there are now two in London. If these are Yau's answer to simple, affordable high street dining, then Hakkasan (Hakka is a Chinese dialect, San a Japanese form of address) is the glamorous, designer-label one-off.

The discreet location plays a large part in creating breathtaking first impressions of Hakkasan. This moody temple of Oriental chic is tucked in down a back alley with a junkie past in London's West End. The unassuming, speakeasy-style street entrance forms part of the seduction, as it reveals barely a hint of the exquisite netherworld below. The restaurant is entirely subterranean, and diners descend a dim staircase studded with ankle-high, deep red lights to emerge in the reception of the 130-cover restaurant and cocktail bar. Hakkasan specializes in modern Cantonese food, serving Dim Sum by day and à la carte by night.

Like a theatrical impresario, Yau is a great believer in setting the scene, the greater the anticipation the better. 'A basement of that size needs a little bit of surprise and what's nice about the winding staircase is the dramatic effect,' he explains. 'So you see nothing from the street level, but as you walk down the stairs you get a glimpse of the beauty of the place, such as the very rich material lining the stairs, the green Burlington stone along with the dark, low recessed light boxes. When you arrive in the basement it hits you straight away; the arrival route creates a wow factor.' Diners enter a single-height reception area, brightened up by a row of pink orchids and the smell of incense. The restaurant is visible directly ahead, although the magnitude of the space only unfolds as diners enter the main arena.

Left:
The 16 metre (52 foot) oak bar runs parallel to the dining cage, to the left of which is a 60-seater cocktail lounge.

Right:
A view through the dining area to the bar and layered black slate wall beyond.

Opposite:
Antique screens from Taipei have been integrated into the oak cage structure.

Above right:
Beyond the cage lie the lounge bar and luminescent blue light panels.

Yau's ambition was to produce a modern ethnic restaurant that embodies traditional Chinese ornamentation in a contemporary style. Hakkasan is a deliberate departure from the clean white minimalism prevalent in London's modern Chinese restaurants. Liaigre's task was to 'bring back the dragon'; this he has achieved (with assistance from UK architects Jestico + Whiles) in a monumental way.

The cavernous, double-height (very Manhattan) space is dominated by a floor-to-ceiling dark timber cage that encloses the dining area. 'Christian found a set of antique screens in Taipei,' recalls Yau; 'he bought the whole lot and integrated them into the dark English oak cage structure to form a partition between areas.' Access routes run through and around the outsides of the screens; the kitchen is on the same level, set behind clear and opaque glass.

The heavy, dark wood screens are elevated and silhouetted against iridescent cobalt-blue light panels adorning the perimeter walls. Devised by Isometrix lighting technician Arnold Chan, these bestow a calm, submarine sensation to the interior, further enhanced by the rippling, watery effect across the roughly sawn, layered slate back wall by lighting projectors. Yau originally wanted to grow real moss on this wall, but this was logistically impossible in a basement; Liaigre opted instead for moving, dappled light to add drama.

A 16 metre (52 foot) dark-stained oak bar with an illuminated blue glass façade runs along the rear of the space, parallel to the dining cage. To the left of the dining enclosure is a 60-seater cocktail lounge furnished with low, marble-topped tables and baby blue leather furniture custom designed by Liaigre and manufactured in France. This is where the dragon truly reigns: the back of each chair is emblazoned with a fiery embroidered dragon motif.

Since opening, Hakkasan has won numerous design awards, appeared in a scene in the hit movie *About a Boy* and in 2003 became the first Chinese restaurant in the UK (and the fifth ever) to earn one Michelin star.

Amar has created an interior that carries DJ Challe's message loud and clear; the divine trinity of music, food and love equals Nirvana

The view from the dining
mezzanine level shows that
nothing is left unadorned:
Nirvana's surfaces glitter with
decoration; walls are a riot of
pink, covered with mirrored
mosaic tiles and other
custom-crafted details.

Encircling the mezzanine are
cosy dining dens, furnished
with lotus-shaped chairs and
decorated with Hindu deities.

Nirvana, Paris, France
March 2002
Amar Design

Hip Paris restaurant-discotheque Nirvana offers
diners a kitsch trip into a pop-exotic fantasyland. From the
minute you step through the door, senses are awakened
by the scent of incense and a ceiling blooming with pink
roses. Located in the exclusive 8th Arrondissement, close
to designer boutiques such as Chanel and Dior, Nirvana
attracts a suitably haute, cosmopolitan clique. The interior,
described as 'an Indian Palace reinvented in a
psychedelically modern guise', was created by French
designer Jonathan Amar, who based his concept on
'gentle bliss'. Nirvana's owners are the prolific Paris
restaurateur Thierry Bourdoncle and his stellar partner, the
'Jet Set's Pied Piper', DJ Claude Challe.

Challe is the legendary musical force behind
Les Bains Douches superclub and ultra-cool *boîte*, the
Buddha Bar and its best-selling eponymous lounge music
CDs. Amar's interior is the visual embodiment of Challe's
music, which 'fuses exotic, heavily atmospheric world
grooves together with cutting-edge dance music'. Amar
has blended similarly far-fetched design styles and
influences: 'the inventive and free spirit of Goa in its heyday
with Pop effervescence, a high-tech futuristic quality and
elements borrowed from traditional Indian style'.

First, all internal structures of an existing restaurant and club were demolished in order to install an acoustic shell (essentially a concrete box placed on spring mechanisms by architect Olivier Billotte) and reorganize the space. On the ground floor is the fine dining restaurant and bar, and in the basement there is a more relaxed dining lounge, bar and dance floor that metamorphoses post 11 p.m. into a club.

The restaurant displays 'the voluptuous comfort of a low Indian salon'. Indian-inspired chairs and long, curvaceous divans in silky plum upholstery were custom-designed and manufactured in Amar's Moroccan workshops. Flamboyant pendant globes light this area like colourful, floating balloons. Reclaimed antique carved wooden arches housing space-enhancing mirrors add a dose of Eastern authenticity.

Right:
The heart-shaped bar glows with hot colours beneath crystal glass lighting by Thomas Bastide.

A beating heart-shaped bar is at the core of the room, 'to give a psychedelic rhythm'. Fabricated from luminous glass panels separated by strips of hammered copper, it is backlit to glow with hot colours from orange to fuchsia. Futuristic ovoid bar stools in pearly pink sit well on a plum-coloured resin floor. Glass artisan Thomas Bastide collaborated with Amar to create blown-crystal glass lighting in orange, pink and plum, and wall lights that echo the heart theme. Semicircular brackets filled with Baccarat crystal are illuminated to emulate a pink 'crushed-ice' effect in which red crystal hearts shine out.

Left:
In the Indian Salon restaurant, pink and mauve drapes and blinds are drawn at night or during bad weather.

Opposite

Left:
An illuminated aquarium conceals the DJ booth in the basement lounge club.

Centre:
Neon hearts and stars light up the poptastic bar downstairs, which is adjacent to the flashing dance floor.

Right:
Those seeking Nirvana get down on a giant vinyl disc.

Towards the rear a small flight of stairs leads up to a balcony and mezzanine level with metal-topped tables and rose Plexiglas chairs. Encircling this open area are more exotic, intimate dining areas asparkle with pretty confectionery details. Lilac-pink walls and columns glitter with silver mouldings and intricate mosaics. Pierre Mesguich created the floral motifs and Aude Pichard the geometric friezes. Ornate archways lead through to cosy nooks and crannies with colourful, lotus-shaped armchairs and walls adorned by engravings and pictures of Hindu divinities. The fuchsia-lacquered rear dining room, framed by antique Indian arcades, is furnished with retro 1970s-style purple sofas and club chairs designed by Amar, and plasma screens as artworks.

A marble staircase descends along a blue wall encrusted with mirrored floral mosaic, down to the lounge and club. This is far more futuristic in ambience, Challe says: 'You think you are walking in paradise, it's more Zen because the lighting will change colour.' Amar has bathed the space in neon lighting of changing colours radiating from holes punctuating the ceiling and support columns, 'designed to give those who abandon themselves here the feeling of vibrating, floating in a rhythm of sound and colour'. The lighting system by Axys generates numerous different tones and atmospheres, from a slowly changing rainbow effect to stroboscopic lighting when the atmosphere is more electric. Pure white banquette seating, as low and deep as beds, soaks up the diffuse colours in the sunken lounge area.

An illuminated aquarium conceals the DJ booth, and the adjacent bar features an orange glass front lit by optical fibre hearts and stars. Patrons dance on a huge vinyl disc surrounded by mirrored walls bearing gigantic 'frequency bars', light strips that flash in time to the beat generated by the state-of-the-art sound system. Amar has created a rose-tinted interior that transmits DJ Challe's message loud and clear: the divine trinity of music, food and love equals Nirvana.

Inside El Japonès the stark simplicity conveys a sense of modern Oriental serenity

El Japonès, Barcelona, Spain
August 1999
Sandra Tarruella and Isabel Lopez

Over the past decade the restaurant scene in Western developed countries has been influenced considerably by Asian culture: some say that Asian food, especially Japanese dishes such as noodles and sushi, is so popular that it is 'the new Italian'. Barcelona's El Japonès restaurant, owned by Grupo Tragaluz, offers diners a fusion menu, described as 'sushi à la Mediterranean'.

Designers Sandra Tarruella and Isabel Lopez have created an interior to complement this hybrid cuisine. Their sparse, almost Zen-like space is their interpretation of an Eastern aesthetic constructed from Spanish materials. 'It was about evoking in diners a memory of heir own perspective on the Japanese culture, derived from movie images, art, contemporary Japanese architecture, documentaries and places.' Tarruella and Lopez are great believers in working with the existing structure of a building: 'We try to use a design vocabulary suitable for each space ... the famous phrase of André Gide would apply, "That art thrives on restrictions and dies with liberty".' The Barcelona-based duo applied this philosophy to El Japonès, letting the existing structures dictate the restaurant layout.

The façade was inspired by Peter Greenaway's film *The Pillow Book*. Large sticks of bamboo sprout from window boxes signalling the entrance. The gleaming door, clad in silver-leaf, bears discreet signage and is framed by two protruding monolithic slabs – a second one was added to create symmetry. Clear glazing either side of the central doorway reveals views of the restaurant; below knee-level, brown rice has been poured into a clear cavity to conceal the undersides of the front benches. A pair of eye-catching Ingo Maurer Zettelz lamps hangs above the front tables, reinforcing the harmonious symmetry of the façade.

Inside El Japonès the stark simplicity conveys a sense of modern Oriental serenity. Tarruella and Lopez have struck a refined balance between cold metals and warm woods, with shimmering silver and matt zinc, and an abundance of grey against shiny, pepper red. It's a space of carefully considered contrasts: 'The use of straight/ structured and austere shapes, the combination of warm and cold materials, the contrast of colours and textures, matts and glosses, all reflect a Japanese style', they explain.

The dining-room walls are clad in 'fish-scale' zinc panelling, except for the partition wall, which is faced with a single piece of silver metal mesh measuring 24 metres (79 feet) long and 3.5 metres (11 feet 6 inches) high. Dividing pillars perpendicular to this wall reduce echo and create intimacy for patrons dining *à deux*. They also contain air-conditioning ducting, as does the false ceiling: such components are concealed throughout to give a clean, uncluttered space.

The open kitchen runs parallel to the dining room, enriching the space with its fiery red interior. The walls are ablaze with shiny red mosaic tiles, repeated in the restrooms, chosen for their strong visual resonance with Japanese enamels. Patrons have various dining options: they may sit at smaller tables along the mesh wall on benches at communal tables, or alone at the sushi bar overlooking the kitchen action.

Tarruella and Lopez's sparse palette of materials has a strong impact: 'The use of solid, oiled wood flooring, the rows of benches, as well as the silver leaf on false ceiling and zinc panels, give the place that desired formal character, open and dynamically transient.' Chunky blocks of iroko wood furniture certainly lend warmth to what would otherwise be quite a brutal, cold space. Choosing the dining chairs to suit wasn't easy either: 'it was difficult to choose a chair with enough personality so as not to be drowned with its context'. However, the pair took their cue from Japanese architect Tadao Ando and opted for his favourite, Hans Wegner's CH-24 chair. Pepe Cortez's Jamaican stool also seemed to fit perfectly with the look, summarized best by Tarruella and Lopez: 'we used little expression, but heaps of visual strength'.

Left:
The clean, uncluttered look is maintained by the concealment of services within support pillars and above the silver ceiling.

Right:
Ingo Maurer's Zettelz lamps were chosen specifically by the designers because 'they have little pages covered in annotations, reminiscent of those used as offerings in Buddhist temples'.

Far right:
The silver mesh functions as an acoustic resonator, as well as a soundproof buffer protecting the adjacent property.

WasabiSabi is a venue of two halves, offering Hong Kong urbanites a cutting-edge restaurant and a chichi lounge bar in one

Left:
Rings of downlit ball chains
hang along the periphery of
the Lipstick Lounge.

WasabiSabi, Hong Kong, China
April 2002
Glamorous & David Yeo

WasabiSabi is a venue of two halves, offering Hong Kong urbanites a cutting-edge Japanese restaurant and a chichi metropolis lounge bar in one. Owner David Yeo explains: 'The "lounge dining" concept of WasabiSabi aims to bring a seamless integration of bar, dining and late night, chill-out lounge.' It is also East meets West: 'the design deliberately unfolds two concepts, seamlessly going from a contemporary Western influence (the bar and Lipstick Lounge) to a contemporary Eastern influence (the sushi and tatami private dining room)'. The 650 square metre (7,000 square foot) site is located on the 13th floor, above one of Hong Kong's busiest shopping malls in Causeway Bay, an area comparable to London's West End and known for its fashion stores, restaurants and nightlife.

Equipped with a $1.5-million budget, Yeo collaborated with Yasumichi Morita and Satomi Hatanaka of the acclaimed Tokyo-based design company Glamorous to create WasabiSabi. It accommodates 120 diners in booths, on tables for two, on communal tables and at a sushi bar; the lounge bar seats 60 drinkers. Patrons enter via a glowing catwalk defined by shimmering columns of light. These are downlights encircled by rings of ball chains cascading from the ceiling; the mirrored ceiling adds a sense of depth and intensifies the illumination. This glittering pathway effectively divides the restaurant from the bar.

However, the real wizardry of WasabiSabi is the row of swivelling booths, the backs of which line the catwalk to enclose the restaurant and separate the dining area from the entrance and bar. These rosewood veneer booths, with black vinyl upholstered seats, rotate a full 360 degrees. At 10.30 p.m. they are swung round by 180 degrees and become part of the candlelit, red velvet Lipstick Lounge, which is open until 3 a.m. Friday and Saturday. The centrepiece of the Lipstick Lounge is the 25 metre (82 foot) long, V-shaped bar, lit by a lightbox that mirrors the line of the bar. Fabricated from acrylic, it bears the WasabiSabi logo constructed in laser-cut film and resembles Japanese 'washi' paper. Spotlights emanating from the lightbox are reflected in the highly polished black granite countertop.

Above left:
The glittering entrance corridor marks a clean white line between the muted dining area and the red velvet of the lounge bar.

Left:
Swivelling rosewood-veneered booths, furnished with black vinyl seats, are rotated later every evening to become part of the lounge.

Opposite:
Highly polished granite countertops provide glossy, reflective surfaces.

By contrast, the restaurant area is calm and subdued, the lighting generally low. Walls are either matt black or mirrored, and floors are finished in black and green natural slate to complement the colour palette of black and wasabi green. The interior is clean and pared down, almost Zen-like, with timber tatami mat-topped tables and simple, chrome-steel-framed furniture upholstered in black or brown leather. The backlit rear wall of the sushi bar features a delicate, organic decoration: banyan branches set behind frosted glass are dramatically underlit to throw ghostly silhouettes of this ancient Asian tree against the glass.

Running parallel to the swivelling booths on the restaurant side are two long communal tables. Each seats 20 diners and is lit by a column of large, square lanterns suspended from the ceiling above. These lanterns serve to enhance the 'phantom' height and infinite depth created by the mirrors on the ceiling and at either end of the communal tables. In the Tatami private dining room this space-enhancing effect is repeated through the use of undulating steel plates covered with crushed velvet, again repeated ad infinitum into the distance by wall mirrors.

At Tuscan, JBI have captured the spirit of northern Italy in a very New York way

Tuscan, New York, USA

December 2000

Jeffrey Beers International

There is something inherently New York about Tuscan (formerly Tuscan Steak), a fine dining northern Italian restaurant located in Manhattan's midtown business district. The soaring space and sheer grandiosity of the main dining room are quintessentially Big Apple: it is a 21st-century banqueting hall designed by Jeffrey Beers International to entertain the 'Masters of the Universe'. New York-based consultancy JBI renovated 650 square metres (7,000 square feet) of the basement and ground floor of an office building and transformed it into this monumental restaurant by adding a mezzanine level and grand staircase connecting the three floors. Tuscan accommodates over 300 people and encompasses six environments: the main dining room, adjoining 'platform' dining area and mezzanine bar inhabit the ground floor, while the basement houses two private dining rooms, a bar and lounge, plus the kitchens and restrooms.

A generous use of natural materials such as wenge wood, marble and bronze, combined with the grand scale and geometry of the design, bestows a rich classicism upon the ground-floor restaurant. JBI took their cues from the food, looking to Tuscany and Milan for inspiration, hence the warm, rustic tones of the interior. Patrons enter a slender lobby area, which houses the reception desk, cloakroom and wenge wood, blackened steel and glass staircase. A colourful mosaic floor constructed from large marble slabs in earthy hues of numidian red, giallo sienna, yellow ramon and crème fedora paves the way.

The entrance area is concealed behind one of two towers that book-end the main dining room. The 'art glass' tower at the entrance displays images of Etruscan stone walls printed onto translucent film and laminated between two layers of glass. The grand, glowing tower at the opposite end of the restaurant mirrors this structure but is constructed from steel, clad in bronze and polished black nickel with Le Mystère glass vitrines to display the wine. Each bottle is fixed on custom brackets of polished stainless steel. The glass was chosen for its 'two-faced' quality: the vitrines are transparent from the front but translucent from the side, so the appearance of the tower alters according to the angle of the viewer.

The irregular grid and rectangles of the towers are a recurring motif throughout the scheme, from the marble mosaic floor of the entrance to the lighting fixtures of the main dining room. These shimmering, oblong installations consist of a series of candelabra and louvred par lamps surrounded by bronze bead fringing of varying lengths. The window dressing reveals the source of this geometric theme: the vast storefront glazing has been draped in double-layered sheer fabric panels in hues of gold, copper and champagne. Suspended from bronze beads spaced 18 centimetres (7 inches) apart, these create an effect intentionally reminiscent of Mondrian's abstract 'composition' paintings.

The ground-floor restaurant seats just under 200 diners, on beige dining chairs and a series of U-shaped black 'liquid leather' booths lining the perimeter of the room. This colour palette is echoed in the bateig blanca limestone floor with absolute black granite inserts. The mezzanine, constructed from two vast horizontal slabs, occupies half of the space: clad in solid wenge wood, these enhance the room's grandeur and sense of luxury. On the upper level is the bar, with glass guardrails affording clear views of the restaurant. Below this, adjoining the main dining room, is the more intimate 'platform dining' area. This seats up to 50 diners, with bold red furniture upholstered in faux ostrich skin and a metal louvred back screen suggesting rural fencing. The ceiling lights in this area are custom resin and perforated metal cylindrical fixtures inserted into white resin shields.

Counterbalancing the colossal scale of the main features, elegant floor and table lamps with stems of alternating Carrara marble and bronze rings topped by linen shades are dotted around the space. Through an intelligent use of quality materials and an autumnal palette, JBI have captured the spirit of northern Italy in a very New York way.

Left:
The art glass 'Etruscan stone' tower at one end conceals the staircase behind but also incorporates the balcony access route to the mezzanine level.

Right:
In the entrance area, large marble floor slabs, in earthy hues of numidian red, giallo sienna, yellow ramen and crème fedora, pave the way.

Far right:
Custom resin and perforated metal fixtures, inserted in white resin shields, light the raised dining area.

'I wanted to introduce the idea of magic and relaxation,' says Jouin of his enchanted garden at Spoon Byblos

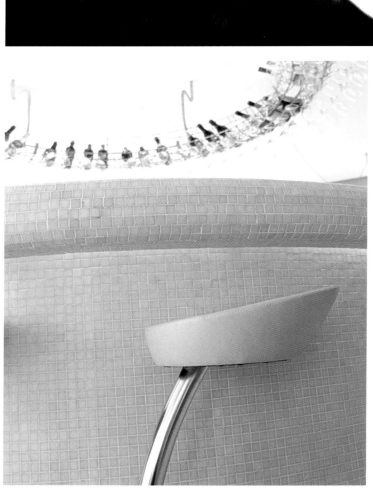

Spoon Byblos, Saint-Tropez, France
April 2002
Patrick Jouin

In the 21st century it is no longer enough for Michelin star chefs to preside over one or two dining establishments: they've gone global. French chef Alain Ducasse's gastronomic empire spans three continents. Eponymous restaurants aside, Spoon Byblos is the Saint-Tropez outpost of a dining concept Ducasse launched in Paris in 1998. His 'spoonful of freedom and a multi-ethnic cuisine' was so successful that there are now Spoons in Mauritius, London and Tokyo.

The Byblos hotel resort, where Spoon is located, is modelled on a colourful Mediterranean hillside village. It was built in 1967, in response to Saint-Tropez's new-found international status as the summer destination for the world's jet set. Ideal then that the Spoon concept offers 'Mediterranean rim' food, with Provençal, Italian, Catalan, Andalusian and Moroccan influences.

Ducasse appointed his preferred partner in design, fellow Frenchman Patrick Jouin, to create the 250-cover restaurant. Jouin took his cue from the food and looked to the Mediterranean countries from Spain, Italy and the South of France to Morocco and Tunisia for inspiration. And since Saint-Tropez is all about the summer and dining alfresco, his main aim was 'to connect the outside and inside' – hence the continuation of the teak parquet floor from inside the restaurant through the large bay windows and out onto the vast outdoor terrace.

The majority of tables at Spoon are dotted around this leafy terrace. Low, cotton-covered ottomans, with adjustable back-rests sporting Moroccan orange backs, replace standard dining chairs. 'I wanted to introduce the idea of magic and relaxation,' says Jouin of his enchanted garden; 'people dine differently in Saint-Tropez in summer than in Paris. It's hot; even if it's a good restaurant your attitude is more laid back; that's why I created the low ottomans.' This lounge mode of dining also suits the Spoon menu, which is designed for sharing.

Above and above left:
Jouin chose lights by Artemide for the leather-lined VIP dining area: 'They're a little bit weird and sexy, and I'd never seen them in a restaurant before.'

Left and far left:
Details of the bar, with its specially designed, UFO-like glass rack above.

Left:
Storm lanterns hanging from tree branches and candles in small glass jugs light the tables in the garden.

It was important that Jouin create an enticing restaurant interior for Spoon Byblos: 'In Saint-Tropez it's better to be outside, but then the restaurant would be empty, which is not good.' The refreshing centrepiece of the interior is the circular bar, clad in blue molten glass mosaic tiles so that it appears to curve up organically from the floor. 'This was inspired by the courtyard fountain you find in Moroccan houses. I like the idea of the blue creating an icy, fresh place in the centre of the restaurant. The sun has been beating down all day and you need somewhere cool to drink,' explains Jouin.

The bar is crowned by a specially designed glass rack, which Jouin compares to a UFO. A constellation of simple pendant lamps arranged in orbit formation around this focal point resemble flying-saucer satellites and light the surrounding area.

If the bar isn't enough to tempt patrons inside, Jouin has created a luxurious VIP dining room lined in sumptuous, saddle-stitched burgundy leather. 'I wanted to convey the idea of Morocco and Hermès', says Jouin, 'so you have this almost red North African leather, but it's stitched so the overall look is very chic.' He also treated the ceiling to 20 coats of lacquer to produce the shiny, rich reflective quality.

In his quest to create unique restaurant interiors Jouin prefers to design the chairs; Spoon Byblos is no exception to the rule.

Above:
Moroccan lanterns provide additional lighting in the bar, while cool blue light floods in through the floor-to-ceiling internal windows that reveal the wine storage.

Plan:
Most of the dining at Spoon Byblos is alfresco on low tables scattered about the terrace; the interior features an island bar and a leather-lined dining room.

With the name Wildfire you know it's not going to be some place with white walls

Wildfire, Sydney, Australia
April 2002
Bucich Studios

Although Sydney's restaurant scene garners praise from around the world, it is a fairly recent phenomenon that has emerged over the past decade. Since the start of the new millennium, harbourside dining in the city has burgeoned, with many designer establishments and restaurants featuring star chefs opening in the Circular Quay vicinity. Wildfire joins a bevy of destination venues that occupy the redeveloped Overseas Passenger Terminal on the west side of the Quay. Owned by New Zealander Tonci Farac, it's the younger sibling of Auckland's Brazilian-inspired Wildfire Churrascaria and serves wood-fired food created by renowned chef Mark Miller. Wildfire accommodates 350 diners and attracts the business crowd during the day, serious diners on weekday evenings and couples and special occasion diners at the weekend.

The design of Wildfire was a collaborative effort between Farac and local multi-disciplinary architecture and design consultancy Bucich Studios, led by New York-born and trained Thomas Bucich. As Farac explains, he commissioned Bucich Studios to salvage an existing interior scheme: 'I saw a profile on Thomas and his furniture designs in *Vogue* and called him up, because I wasn't happy with certain areas and the colour scheme; Thomas helped consolidate the design and really turn it into something.'

Bucich's design concept is characterized by 'fire and ice': opposite the fiery, open marble kitchen is a cold seafood bar; materials such as white marble and aluminium are offset by a warm, earthy colour palette and flaming red details. 'There were disparate elements in the scheme and I pulled them all together,' explains Bucich, 'drawing on the New Mexican or Santa Fe influence without making it the obvious theme.'

As in the case of neighbouring restaurant Opium (see page 120), city guidelines stipulated that the view of the Opera House from Circular Quay West must be retained. In order to make the space more inviting, two mezzanine floors flank the double-height space, both set 2 metres (6 feet 7 inches) back from the glass façade. One is open, while the other, with part of the main space, is enclosed by glass and reserved for private dining. As for the rich, native Australian jarrah timber floor and burnt reds and oranges of the colour scheme, Farac explains: 'We had to warm it up because of the 7.5 metres (25 feet) of glass. With the name Wildfire you know it's not going to be some place with white walls.'

Three majestic chandeliers, reminiscent of ice crystal creations, crown the dining room, each being three lights in one. 'I looked for two years to find the right lights,' says Farac: 'they had to be large without restricting the view.' They introduce a sense of glamour and grandeur, and also serve to draw the eye through the space to the water and the Opera House beyond. Below the chandeliers a 5 metre (16 foot) long aluminium and wood table forms the dining centrepiece, offering a dozen diners the prime view. Larger groups are also accommodated in the high-backed booths, whereas single diners are best positioned at the seafood bar.

Bucich's aluminium wine storage wall is the other main feature. The simple grid structure is animated by a row of orange poles sprouting up from the floor and piercing the cantilevered ledge that allows access to the upper shelves. 'The imagery is a reference to three elements,' explains Bucich, 'the industrial grid of the terminal, the tree trunk pole configuration of New Mexican Indian kiva ladders and the burning wood of Wildfire's wood-burning and open-flame cooking methods.' These poles are a recurring motif: Bucich has also incorporated them in the aluminium and wood coffee tables in the linear bar that runs parallel to the dining room.

Below:
Tiny flames provide a
flickering frame to views of
the dining room from the bar.

Bottom:
In the Ember bar, the long,
curved timber counter echoes
the form of the marble hood
that arches up over the open
kitchen in the adjoining
dining room.

The textures, hues and forms of the Ember bar lend it a 1960s vibe. Highly polished, dark chocolate Venetian plaster and dark timber are brightened up by cushioned wall-panelling of orange cotton-blend polyester fabric. All the furniture was designed and custom-made for the project. 'Glyde' lounge chairs are upholstered in red and orange neoprene wetsuit fabric: 'it made sense, since there's a lot of splashing in a bar', says Bucich. The long, curved timber bar echoes the form of the marble hood that arches up over the open kitchen in the adjoining dining space. The dividing wall houses open-flame fireplaces surrounded by panels of brushed aluminium, allowing drinkers to glimpse the dining room over rows of tiny flames. Bucich also created exterior furniture for the Ember bar: dark-stained timber sofas and chairs with faux ostrich-leather upholstery.

Retro-Pop

Jones offers diners home-grown familiarity and a buoyant nostalgia

Jones, Philadelphia, USA
September 2002
David Schefer Design

In this age of uncertainty, Philadelphia's Jones restaurant offers diners home-grown familiarity and a buoyant nostalgia. The lofty interior, with its flagstone columns, teak panelling and cork floor, brightened by a retro palette of burnt orange, avocado and light turquoise, evokes the spirit of late-1950s/early-1960s America. Retrospectively labelled the 'atomic age', parallels can be drawn with our current climate of insecurity. Restaurateur Stephen Starr recognizes the instinct to 'return to the hearth' only too well. As New York-based designer David Schefer explains: 'He asked us to create a warm, comfortable and familiar environment to serve stylized American comfort food. Responding to recent world events and the current state of the economy he felt that such an inviting setting would appeal to his customers' mindset.'

Jones occupies the ground floor of an office building on the periphery of Philadelphia's Old City, where trendy bars, restaurants and nightclubs have begun to emerge and flourish. Formerly a retail unit, the 280 square metre (3,000 square foot) site had to undergo considerable renovation to become a 125-cover restaurant. David and Eve-Lynn Schefer added a new staircase to the existing mezzanine level, excavated a sunken area and installed a new shopfront with full-height windows to make the interior open and inviting to passers-by.

At the heart of the restaurant is a sunken rectilinear lounge enclosure, made cosy by a teak ceiling, low teak partitioning and avocado green banquette seating. Anchoring this is a two-sided fireplace, also visible to patrons seated in the diner-style booths by the windows. On the opposite side of the enclosure a row of spiky plants along the top of the teak partition obscures the bar.

The most uplifting feature is the beach scene photomural filling the teak-lined recess behind the bar. 'It was taken on the New Jersey shore during the 1940s,' explains Eve-Lynn Schefer. 'We coloured the balloons in the image to add a quirky touch and tie it into the colour scheme.' White leather bar stools reflect the shiny turquoise blue of the bar counter which, like the tables, is a high-gloss polyester resin.

Light from a variety of different sources brings the scheme to life. Small recessed downlights spot table tops and walkways; elsewhere backlit grass cloth sconces and panels radiate amber warmth and hidden cove lighting emphasizes the texture of the stone columns; this is echoed by similar uplighting sweeping up the perimeter columns to generate an enticing glow around the window-side booths. Dazzling custom-designed chandeliers 'inspired by atomic-age imagery' are the booths' crowning glory. The specially designed night lights, tiny backlit monochrome images of American tourist locations on the perimeter tables, are a delightful detail.

Although in an urban setting, Jones definitely has the whimsical charm of a neighbourhood restaurant. The name says it all, explains David Schefer: 'It was derived from the most common of American last names and chosen for its familiar and generic appeal.' Keeping up with the Joneses never looked so inviting.

Asian-fusion restaurant Pod embodies the optimism of 1960s pop modernism

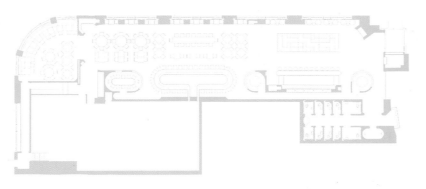

Left:
The dining room at the rear can be made private by drawing across a luminescent curtain of silicon tubing.

Plan:
Rockwell's curvaceous plan is well considered, with a raised area for lounging by the lozenge-shaped bar overlooking the main dining area, as well as several small 'pod' enclosures for private dining parties.

Below:
The front of the space – the lounge area, also known as the 'adult playpen' – is highlighted by a shiny, blood-red construction fabricated from polyurethane-coated foam.

Bottom:
'Deuce pods' line one wall, providing cosy enclosures for two.

Pod, Philadelphia, USA
October 2002
David Rockwell Group

'In 1962, if we decided to design a futuristic restaurant, this is what it would look like. Very clean, very white, sort of Woody Allen's Sleeper meets Kubrick's 2001,' says Philly's restaurant impresario Stephen Starr of Pod. This retro-futuristic Asian-fusion restaurant, located on the University of Pennsylvania campus, embodies the optimism of 1960s pop modernism, augmented by inventive applications of the latest hi-tech materials and technologies. Although attached to a hotel, the 244-seater Pod restaurant and bar operates independently, attracting a trendy crowd including graduate students, visiting business people and affluent local suburbanites.

The name derives from the design: the rectilinear 740 square metre (8,000 square foot) space has been carved into various mini-pods by the New York-based multi-discipline consultancy the Rockwell Group. US *Esquire* magazine's profile of architect David Rockwell ('The People's Architect', March 2002) observed that he loves 'playful fantasies' and wants to 'make the world a stage set where magic things can happen'. Pod is clearly his funky, space-age creation. Predominantly white, with a poured concrete floor, high-gloss white epoxy walls, curvy white moulded fibreglass chairs and white polyester-coated

timber tables, niches and sub-capsules are 'painted' in colours by electronically controlled neon lights.

An 'oval racecourse' ceiling provides the majority of light in the main pod body. The centre of colour-cued acoustical foam-rubber tiles is encircled by backlit lumasite ceiling panels projecting a glowing orange halo above the bar and dining room. Three 1.2 metre (4 foot) diameter neon-lit circles coffered into the foam ceiling appear to hover above the lounge. These are mirrored by concentric rings of coloured light cast by framed overhead projectors onto the floor like 'pop art' targets. Low, custom-made ottomans scattered around the lounge provide surprise illumination: when patrons sit down on cushions (made from the gel used in wheelchair seats) they light up like beacons.

The centrepiece is Rockwell's shiny, red 'adult playpen', or 'barge', a geometric configuration of seating intended as an interactive sculptural piece for 'playing and lounging'. Moulded from polyurethane-coated foam, this soft but resilient material is typically used in water parks. Aligning this is the bar, crowned by a glowing counter of translucent amber resin embedded with white neon lights. White stools with Saarinen-inspired 'tulip' stems, upholstered with 'liquid leather', enhance the futuristic high-gloss aesthetic.

Pod is a capsule of soft curves, circles and lozenges; even the stair handrails that lead down to the dining level are wrapped in escalator rubber. The star attraction is the 'kai ten' sushi bar with a 17 metre (55 foot) long conveyor belt and durable white corian counter. As sushi revolves past, diners seated on low blobular stools select their dishes. Between the sushi bar and the bar are smaller private dining pods. Pure white, these are upholstered in liquid leather and drenched in changing coloured light distributed evenly through the space by the translucent Barrisol ceiling. Elsewhere, dining *à deux* is a cosy affair in the series of 'deuce pods' along the window wall, with their comfortable gel seats.

Tucked towards the rear is a dining room for 48 people. This can be saturated in various colours chosen by the guests or, to add to its ethereal ambience, can be made private by drawing across a luminescent curtain. Fabricated from silicon tubing containing coloured acrylic rods, this is yet another touch of Rockwell's outer space magic.

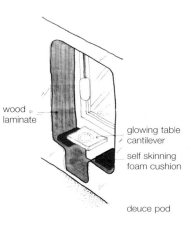

wood laminate
glowing table cantilever
self skinning foam cushion

deuce pod

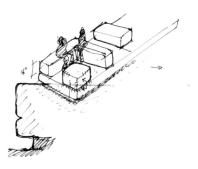

Café Etienne Marcel is the

collaborative creation of two contemporary
artists and a cutting-edge graphic design duo

Left:
At the heart of Café Etienne Marcel is the giant seat-cum-chandelier, suggestive of an upturned udder sprouting smaller udder-shaped bulbs.

Right:
In keeping with the rough 'art-school' aesthetic, splashes of primary colours have been applied randomly to walls, table surfaces and seat cushions.

Café Etienne Marcel, Paris, France
April 2002
Pierre Huyghe, Philippe Parreno &
M/M (Mathias Augustyniak & Michael Amzalag)

As much art installation as restaurant, Café Etienne Marcel belongs to the Costes Brothers' burgeoning empire. Described as Paris's answer to Ian Schrager, brothers Jean-Louis and Gilbert Costes have opened two hotels and a string of successful dining hotspots since launching their legendary Philippe Starck-designed Café Costes in 1983.

Etienne Marcel is the first project to be commissioned by Gilbert Costes's son Thierry. It is open from 8 a.m. until 2 a.m. and is named after its street address in the 2nd arrondissement: as Gilbert Costes says, 'We choose places in rich neighbourhoods, rich in elegance, modernity, creativity or culture' (New York Times, 14 January 2002). Located in a trendy area close to the garment district, it has proved popular with fashionistas and the arterati – unsurprising really, since it's the collaborative creation of two contemporary artists and a cutting-edge graphic design duo.

Avant-garde French artists Pierre Huyghe and Philippe Parreno have worked and exhibited with M/M (graphic design and art direction partnership Mathias Augustyniak and Michael Amzalag) on a number of occasions since 1998. Established in 1992, M/M are currently creative directors for French Vogue and they have also worked for major fashion designers, cultural institutions and pop stars such as Björk and Madonna.

They view their different approaches at Café Etienne Marcel positively: 'The diversity of viewpoints has generated paradoxes, clashes, compromises and a certain degree of complexity in its construction. Hence, several elements compose the Café,' write M/M. A corner site, the physical structure of three previous businesses, has been retained, thus 'providing a "ghost" reference for the treatment of the façade and interior spaces'. The pavement outside has been raised to create exterior window seating for alfresco dining.

Inside, a giant 'chandelier' prototype that appeared in previous exhibitions forms the core of Café Etienne Marcel. A constellation of udder-like bulbs rises up from a shiny central seating cluster to the ceiling, where the bulbs are strung up throughout the space like oversized fairy lights. In the art gallery this light installation functioned like 'a bench in a shopping plaza': it was the central meeting-point and connection between the various works of art by Huyghe, Parenno and M/M exhibited in adjoining rooms. At Etienne Marcel, the spaghetti of black wires supporting the huge bulbs loops through the space like work-lamps on a building site, lending a rough, experimental look to the interior.

This effect is further reinforced by the giant ink-blots decorating the floor and the custom-designed carpet. This bears a wild display of black scribbles, 'in reality a secret and hidden text composed in a typeface designed by a person who cannot read or write', according to M/M.

The simple Formica tables were custom-designed: 'While the table tops could look like square, coloured skateboards, the supporting legs vary. One set of tables bears regular legs, almost like school furniture, while the other set bears "crazy legs", as if there was some action going on underneath.' Huge, shiny moulded fibre-glass chairs, cast from an original late 1960s design (by a Californian urban furniture company) and adapted for interior use, imbue the space with a spacey, retro-futuro feel.

Commissioned to 'design a space of lasting beauty that would ooze a sense of lavish splendour', Mah created Rumi

Opposite:
A view of the dining area from the mezzanine illustrates the sense of drama created by the two levels.

Right:
An illuminated ceiling and bar façade lend a soft glow to the bar area.

Far right:
The golden 'lozenges' play a starring role, providing a contrast in atmosphere between levels, while also unifying the space.

Rumi, Miami, USA
August 2001
Nancy Mah Design

Manhattan-based designer Nancy Mah's projects have earned her the grand title 'Queen of supper club swank' (*Harper's Bazaar*). Her reputation for creating luxurious, louche supper clubs favoured by the beautiful people was born with the launch of Lotus, a hip downtown New York restaurant and club. When Rumi, with its plush, retro-decadent interior, opened in Miami's supercool SoBe district her status was secured. The 560 square metre (6,000 square foot) establishment (named after the 13th-century Middle Eastern poet) includes a small bar and 100-cover restaurant on the ground floor, overlooked by a 250-capacity mezzanine-level cocktail bar and VIP room. Mediterranean- influenced Caribbean food is served in the restaurant and at around midnight the entire space morphs into a late-night lounge club open until 2 a.m.

When Mah was asked to create a room for dining, drinking and spontaneous dancing in a long, narrow space with ceiling heights measuring almost 11 metres (35 feet), a new mezzanine level was the obvious solution. This enabled her to offer customers dining on the ground floor and drinking on the upper level; however, it was vital that both areas would seamlessly flow together for post-midnight partying.

Commissioned to 'design a space of lasting beauty that would ooze a sense of lavish splendour', Mah found inspiration in the sensuous curves of cruise liner and club design of the 1930s and 1940s – a nostalgic style befitting Rumi's location in the 1960s-built Lincoln Road Mall designed by America's godfather of post-war kitsch glamour, Morris Lapidus. Mah's scheme observes many of Lapidus's design rules: use sweeping lines, use light to create unusual effects, try to get drama, keep changing the floor levels and keep people moving.

The cascade of golden Plexiglas lights certainly suggests that Mah shares Lapidus's belief in the 'Moth Complex' theory, that people are attracted to light like moths to a flame. The cluster of 22 light-boxes suspended at different heights dominates the dining area and serves the dual purpose of compressing the volume height to human proportions and, reflected in the mirror-tiled wall that wraps up and over part of the ceiling, adding depth and maximizing the space widthways. Visible from the cocktail lounge above, the golden lozenges encourage a sense of flow between levels and atmospheres.

All the furniture is custom-made for Rumi in a retro-pop colour palette of red and white in the dining room and deep ox-blood red, chocolate and gold in the bar. Curved-edged dining tables resemble Mod targets with their funky red centres of crab shell laid in resin, complemented by red and white curved-back chairs. Large banquettes containing projectors radiate light across the floor. Other groovy light details include internally illuminated cocktail tables that emit a glamorous diffuse light. Softly lit and with plenty of people-watching potential, it's no wonder that Mah's venues are attracting style junkies and the image-conscious crowd like moths to a flame.

Pearl is swathed in an orange and amethyst light, likened by some to a Miami Beach sunset

Pearl Restaurant & Champagne Lounge, Miami, USA
December 2000
Dupoux Design

Since 1988, with the opening of entrepreneur Jack Penrod's Beach Club, Miami's South Beach – SoBe – has flourished into a cool destination for the jet set. Over the past decade French-born designer Stephane Dupoux has played an integral role in glamorizing the district's nightlife. The string of Dupoux-designed restaurants, bars and clubs have become hip, star-studded hangouts and earned him award-winning recognition as a 'sculptor of space'. In 1997 Penrod commissioned Dupoux to create Nikki Beach; a few years later he gave him carte blanche to design a seafood restaurant and champagne lounge bar next door, on the exclusive Ocean Drive. Pearl was the cosmic result.

Right:
There are even a few beds at Pearl, strewn with orange fur cushions.

Far right:
Dupoux's custom-designed Conch chairs are upholstered in white leather to soak up the neon light.

Below:
The 1960s pop polka dot motif is repeated throughout, unifying the interior.

Dupoux decided to go 'all white' and infuse the blank canvas with coloured light. The effect is stunning: Pearl is swathed in an orange and amethyst light, likened by some to a Miami Beach sunset. The perimeter of the 650 square metre (7,000 square foot) interior and the support columns in the restaurant are lined with neon light concealed behind white linen drapes woven with silver thread to transmit the light. 'I used orange neon at the top and purple at the bottom; there is a white fur trim to make the light more diffuse … a bit like a 1960s women's negligee,' he explains. This warm, gentle glow is also, of course, incredibly flattering: 'It gives everybody a tan like they just went to the beach,' says Dupoux. 'Nobody looks tired no matter how hard they party.'

Although the vast space is divided into a 175-cover restaurant (serving multi-cultural fusion food) and a 160-seat lounge, the use of white elements such as the terrazzo floor and leather furniture throughout enhances the sense of flow between areas. The centrepiece of the restaurant is a sunken 'island' bar surrounded by seashell-inspired 'conch' chairs designed by Dupoux, who began his career as a furniture designer. A polka-dot theme creates a sense of continuity: table tops are covered in shiny white epoxy resin with orange polka dots, and white sofas and a corner bed in the lounge are scattered with circular orange fur cushions.

The dining area has white leather chairs with distinctive talon-legs, a detail echoed in the chunky bar stools flanking the long, terrazzo-topped bar in the lounge. A wall of orange- and purple-lit niches houses distinctive 'Nesso' mushroom table lamps (designed by Architetti Urbanista Città Nuova in 1962), adding to the retro-pop aesthetic. Additional furniture created for Pearl includes low polka-dot lounge tables and 'shag ottomans'– cube seats upholstered in orange fur with white leather seats.

A giant 4.9 metre (16 foot) weather balloon is the focus of the orange fur-lined lounge, which has higher ceilings: 'I had to furnish this space carefully,' says Dupoux, 'so I went for an immense pearl hovering overhead to fill the volume.' Black and white visuals projected through orange filters dance on the walls, introducing a psychedelic element. It's no wonder that Pearl's surreal interior has been compared to *Barbarella*, *2001: A Space Odyssey* and *A Clockwork Orange*. But the similarity is entirely coincidental, says Dupoux: 'I've seen none of these movies … I was just experimenting.'

Bed Supperclub's

elliptical tubular construction appears to have been beamed down from another planet

Bed Supperclub, Bangkok, Thailand
August 2002
Orbit Design Studio

Adventurous globetrotters can now recline as they dine in world cities from Asia to America. Huge beds made for sharing are usurping the formalities of tables and chairs in Miami, Amsterdam, London and Rome supperclubs, offering patrons the ultimate in louche dining. One of the latest venues to offer this decadent Bacchanalian experience in spage-age surroundings is Bed Supperclub in Bangkok.

The cosmopolitan collective of contemporary artists, advertising whizz-kids and designers behind the enterprise wanted 'a building that would embody the philosophy of the Bed Supperclub – a modern, stylish, slightly subversive structure'. Orbit Design Studio delivered them a gem: from the street this futuristic, elliptical tubular construction appears to have been beamed down from another planet. Indeed, it has been designed as a transportable construction and can be packed up and moved elsewhere.

The giant, ovoid tube is currently poised in trendy Sukhumvit, a lively area bristling with expat bars and nightlife. Created with a $1-m budget, the structure is based on a technology of aligned rings. The 120-cover restaurant occupies 60 per cent of the 800 square metre (8,600 square foot) interior, with the remainder devoted to a 250-capacity lounge bar.

The restaurant is clearly inspired by Amsterdam's all-white 'Supperclub', with an open kitchen, shiny epoxy resin floor, two broad 'bunks' accommodating vinyl mattresses for laid-back diners and tables in the centre flanked by Panton chairs. Neon hues wash through the space and projections, films and videos play on the white wall above the kitchen, in synchronicity with the DJ who spins discs on a white vintage table.

The separate lounge bar is arranged over two levels with durable corian-topped bars on each, and furnishings of neutral grey, ribbed leather banquettes and cube stools. A glass floor-to-ceiling panel between the levels allows upper-level drinkers a bird's-eye view of fellow lounge lizards below.

At Bed Supperclub's 'surprise weekends', various forms of entertainment, such as performance art or a musical act, are incorporated into the communal 8 p.m. supper. Inhibition-smashing stunts include delivering gooey dessert dishes with rubber gloves as substitutes for cutlery. As Bed Supperclub say, 'we wanted to provide a forum where Bangkok people could meet, exchange ideas and feed off each other creatively in an atmosphere of style and innovation.'

Left:
Bed Supperclub's beds are accessed via a central staircase; the curved walls are padded for comfort and to keep sound levels low and intimate.

Right:
The giant elliptical tube that is Bed Supperclub was designed to be transportable, so that it can 'beam down' elsewhere.

Below:
A glass panel allows views between the restaurant and bar area.

R is a simple open-plan restaurant designed to stand the test of time

Left:
In a room with a view, there's no need for complicated, elaborate design.

Right:
The whitewashed balcony forms a neutral frame to the Paris skyline.

Far right:
In stark contrast to the restaurant, the bar below is almost entirely black, with only Pillet's bright sofas adding colour.

R, Paris, France
May 2002
Christophe Pillet

R restaurant is one of the first commercial interiors completed by hotshot French designer Christophe Pillet. He worked with Martin Bedin in Milan (1986–8) and Philippe Starck in Paris (1988–93) before going solo and earning the prestigious 'Creator of the Year' (*créateur de l'année*) in 1994. Although a cross-discipline designer, he is best known for his furniture and product designs and has collaborated with Cappellini, Artelano and J.C. Decaux, amongst others.

When he was asked to transform an existing restaurant in the quiet, predominantly residential 15th arrondissement of Paris into a 'cool place on a limited budget', he was no doubt grateful for the amazing view. There was no need to create an expensive interior full of grand gestures when the patrons were likely to spend their time gazing outside at the stunning rooftop panorama with the Eiffel Tower in the distance. This enabled him to create a simple open-plan restaurant designed to stand the test of time.

The 350 square metre (3,800 square foot) space comprises two floors: the kitchen, 120-cover dining room and heated open-air terrace on the seventh floor (accessible via a private elevator) and a bar-club and toilets on the sixth floor below. The palette is monochrome, predominantly white in the restaurant and black in the bar below, with accents of primary colour to liven it up. The lounge bar is the nocturnal space, with a black stone floor and walls, a stainless steel and black lacquered bar and even black upholstered furniture (except for the Pillet sofas), all a deliberate contrast to the lighter penthouse restaurant.

In the restaurant support columns and dividing walls are clad in distinctive white-ribbed stucco, lending character without detracting from the view. Surrounding the reception desk and dotted around the restaurant are slender, elongated white plastic vases custom-made by Pillet for the project. Sprouting various leaves and foliage, these appear as live, natural sculptures adding colour to the space.

The furniture is stark white against the black stone floor; the dining chairs are fittingly the Eames DKR classic with 'Eiffel Tower' base, a shape echoed in the skyline vista outside. In order to retain a relatively uncluttered look Pillet has used the simple wire-frame version of the chair in the centre of the room, with red seat cushions engendering warmth. Low sofas designed by Pillet and produced by Venitex, upholstered in bright green and red, add strong splashes of colour.

The heated balcony has whitewashed floors and pure white furniture, forming a blank canvas or clean backdrop against the spectacular view. It is out on deck, dining alfresco, that the restaurant's enigmatic name becomes clear: in French the letter R is pronounced 'Air'.

Chedi Lounge is a café, lounge

diner and cocktail bar wrapped into one

Chedi Lounge, Offenbach, Germany
February 2001
Pur Pur GmbH

During the 1990s that very American creation, 'cocktail culture', swept back into fashion in most cosmopolitan world cities and with it came the lounge, a relaxed, louche environment furnished with casual seating. Lounge dining venues are more often than not a blend of café and bar or restaurant and club. Forget the formality of gourmet restaurants: these hip transitional venues often place as much emphasis on the thriving bar scene as the dining. One of the key reasons for their emergence is the necessity for venues to operate from early in the morning to post-midnight, in order to make a profit.

Offenbach's Chedi Lounge is open from 9 a.m. to 2 a.m. and exhibits all the elements of a lounge diner. The small 174 square metre (1,900 square foot) corner site accommodates 75 seated patrons, typically aged between 18 and 35, and is a café, lounge diner and cocktail bar wrapped into one. During the day it offers customers breakfast, coffee and light snacks; in the evening there is a bistro dinner menu, cocktails are served at the bar and it becomes increasingly clubby as the night wears on. Design agency Pur Pur says that 'the idea was to create different moods over the course of the day with the changing menu, different music styles and most importantly the lighting'.

During the summer the glass doors open out and alfresco seating is provided with white tables and distinctive pink Verner Panton chairs. The matt white oval bar is the main focus and functions to divide the space into three separate areas, each offering slightly different seating options. Individual diner booths line the rear wall and on the left a raised platform housing a banquette and long communal slate-topped table runs parallel to the bar. On the opposite side of the bar is a more conventional dining area, with tables and chairs and two large, C-shaped booths.

Like many 21st-century designers, it was Pur Pur's intention to create a blank canvas and use light to change the environment: 'The colour scheme is very clean and minimalist, to create a sense of space and let the light effects unfold'. Hence the plain, terrazzo-style floor (Estrazzo by Rockies, it features stones covered with resin) and abundance of white surfaces – indeed, the violet of the vinyl ribbed banquettes is the only splash of colour. Coloured neon tubes concealed in recessed elements behind booths and in the oval ceiling structure above the bar wash the space with different hues. Silver Surfer lamps by Brainbox direct extra light onto table tops.

The furniture is sleek and simple; the stainless steel and dark wood chairs and bar stools are by La Palma. Ergonomic curves play a major role: 'All built-in wall or ceiling elements, as well as the furniture, play with organic round shapes which creates a floating as well as flowing atmosphere.' Combined with the artificial lighting, this also makes for a mellow, futuristic vibe.

Opposite:
Groups of diners are accommodated at two large booths that adjoin the more conventional dining tables and chairs.

Below left:
A variety of levels and a range of seating offer slightly different dining and drinking experiences at Chedi Lounge.

Below right:
The white oval bar is central to the space and clearly visible from the broad, glazed front.

Modern Classic

Frankfurt's sleek, modern Coconut Groove accommodates three venues in one: a café, a cocktail bar and a restaurant

Coconut Groove, Frankfurt, Germany
April 2002
Bender Design

Frankfurt's sleek, modern Coconut Groove accommodates three venues in one: a café, a cocktail bar and a restaurant. Its name inspired by a district of Miami, Florida, the connection is reflected in its 'New World' cuisine, described as 'high-end Miami style inspired by food from the Caribbean, California and the Far East'.

Due to its location, on the main thoroughfare Kaiserstrasse, it was important for the design to address the diverse nature of this pocket of the city. The challenge for Bender Design was how to satisfy a broad spectrum of customers, from office workers and tourists by day to culture vultures and clubbers by night. They were commissioned to renovate the early-20th-century site and transform it into a venue, regularly open from 11 a.m. to 3 a.m., comprising an espresso bar, a cocktail bar and a restaurant serving lunch and dinner for a budget of €500,000 ($585,000). 'The general idea was to let the areas melt and flow together, communicating the continuity but without them losing their own character,' explain Bender Design, 'As in Frankfurt, here the "Main" river flows along, but it's a mirrored line that connects the areas and leads us through the restaurant.'

The glass frontage reveals the deep but narrow 180 square metre (1,940 square foot) interior of Coconut Groove to passers-by. In summer the doors fold back and the café spills out onto the pavement, where patrons sit on Tom Vac chairs designed by Ron Arad. Inside, the dynamic red coffee-station protrudes towards the entrance like the bow of a ship. Bender Design developed this eye-catching, futuristic kiosk for take-away coffees; by night it becomes part of the cocktail bar, stretching 11 metres (36 feet) into the space. Both countertops are a composite sandwich of fibreglass reinforced plastic with a polyurethane foam core, lacquered with shiny, coral orange automotive enamel. This brightly coloured structure connects the café/bar with the cocktail lounge and the restaurant beyond: 'The bar is pushed into the lounge area creating this transition between aperitif and meal.'

Colour is used effectively throughout to distinguish and connect different areas. As patrons move through to the lounge, the light grey of the epoxy resin floor gives way to dark-stained timber floorboards. Here the space is compressed to create a sense of intimacy, the ceiling lowered and the floor raised to form a seating platform. The coral colour of the ceiling in this area links it with the bar opposite. An illuminated glass display case containing wine and cigars, set into the back wall and interspersed with paintings by local artists, forms a horizontal break between coral above and timber below. The lighting throughout is recessed or integrated into the furniture and fittings for a refreshing, modern look.

In the slender restaurant space at the rear the colour scheme reverts back to light grey flooring and olive green high-backed banquettes. Tableware is stored in a long timber cupboard set against the wall separating the restaurant from the service areas. The glass rear door opens onto a terrace, and the back wall is clad in crushed aluminium sheet lit dramatically in red, fittingly bringing Coconut Groove to an end with a stunning blaze of coral.

Opposite:
The shiny, coral-orange countertops are made of fibreglass-reinforced plastic, with a polyurethane foam core, and are lacquered with automotive enamel.

Right:
The lighting throughout is recessed or integrated into the furniture and fittings for a refreshing, modern look.

Far right:
Funky, chocolate brown Plank chairs have been used throughout; Millefoglie furnish the restaurant and Bábá armchairs the lounge.

The clean forms of Monastrell's street elevation are, true to Modernist form, a clear indication of what is to come inside

Opposite:
Natural light floods into the
restaurant through the glass
aperture above the entrance.

Plan and elevation:
The kitchen and toilets are
located at the rear of the
L-shaped space.

Above right:
The reception area, with its
iroko wood counter, doubles
as the restaurant holding bar,
with bottles neatly stored to
maintain its clean lines.

Below right:
The iroko wood panelling
adds warmth to an otherwise
stark white interior.

Monastrell, Alicante, Spain,
April 2001
Javier García-Solera Vera

The stark anonymity of Monastrell's silver
aluminium and glass façade engenders a sense of intrigue.
Only subtle embossed signage announces the name of the
establishment, which is taken from the local main grape
variety – used for making reds, rosés and sweet aged
wines. Although the interior is concealed, the clean
horizontal and vertical forms of the street elevation are, true
to Modernist form, a clear indication of what is to come
inside. The restaurant is the work of Spanish architect
Javier García-Solera Vera, who is responsible for several
other architectural projects in Alicante.

García-Solera Vera's brief was to 'create a quiet,
comfortable space where patrons could escape from the
outside noise and enjoy high-quality cuisine'. Hence the
discreet façade: although located on a busy street close
to Alicante's thriving harbour, nobody can glimpse inside
unless the front door is open. The sense of escape has
been achieved without jeopardizing the loss of natural light,
thanks to a horizontal glass aperture above the entrance.

The clean architectural lines of the exterior
continue inside without interruption, defined by the
architect's sparse, pared down palette of materials: iroko
wood, natural stone and aluminium. At the entrance, the
reception counter is constructed from a low block of iroko
wood, whilst wine storage is provided by discreet shelving
set flush in the wall.

The rectilinear 100 square metre (1,080 square
foot) space has been organized simply. The single access
route running from the entrance to the restrooms and
kitchen at the rear is defined by polished grey stone
paving. In contrast, a layer of warm iroko wood envelopes
the dining area: García-Solera Vera has extended this rich
surface from the floor to the wall, creating a timber layer
stretching the length of the room.

Up to 34 diners are accommodated at white
linen-covered tables on matching white plastic chairs by
Philippe Starck. An aluminium ceiling grid echoes the silver
plane of the façade, and affixed to this is a series of
spotlights directed to accent each table top. The lighting
elsewhere is subtle and discreet: corners are lit by standard
lamps with cylindrical paper shades, and recessed lighting
concealed behind the wood panelling emits a diffuse light
projected onto the band of white wall. Perfectly level with
the rectangular glass pane above the door, this appears
the logical extension of natural light and reinforces the
simple Modernist aesthetic.

Vintage 1950s white Murano glass lamps inject Lupino with a dose of retro style

Opposite:
Glass doors at the rear open out onto a terrace that seats a further 40 diners during the summer months.

Below:
The dark-blue resin catwalk guides patrons through the various parts of Lupino.

Lupino, Barcelona, Spain
February 2002
Studiox Design Group

An increasing trend in cosmopolitan cities across the globe is to create multi-purpose venues, designed to accommodate people throughout the day, from 9 a.m. breakfast through to lunch and dinner, ending with cocktails and dancing until 3 a.m. Lupino is one such venue, located behind the Boqueria market and beside the Rambla in Barcelona's popular Ciutat Vella neighbourhood, the old part of town, which thrives with trendy locals and tourists flocking there for the bars, restaurants, galleries and museums.

Prior to the renovation it was a shop. 'It was a large, open loft-like space, with only pillars and the mezzanine,' Studiox architect Ellen Rapelius explains. 'The client showed us many places, but when we saw this place we fell in love with it immediately, even though we were conscious it was quite a difficult shape for renovation.' The Barcelona-based architects were asked to transform the long, thin 350 square metre (3,770 foot) space into a venue including a café lounge, cocktail bar, chill-out area, restaurant and terrace for a budget of €360,000 ($420,000).

Studiox achieved the brief through an intelligent organization of space. The 50 metre (164 foot) long site is narrow, measuring 4 to 7 metres (13 to 23 feet) wide; the ceiling height increases to include a mezzanine towards the rear entrance/exit. 'It's like an aeroplane,' says Rapelius: 'the existing structure gave us the idea to design a long, brilliant blue catwalk, running the entire length of the place taking patrons past all the different areas and leading to the staircase.' In order to retain 'perception and visibility' throughout the entire space, Studiox placed the office and restrooms upstairs and tucked the kitchen into a narrow space on one side. The café-lounge is at the front, followed by the bar and then the chill-out area; towards the rear is the restaurant.

A perforated plasterboard ceiling was installed for acoustic absorption: 'The height of this ceiling changes in every area and draws a sinuous line with rounded edges adapting itself to the special needs of every area'. Studiox also used colour to define the space, connecting the different areas with the dark-blue resin catwalk and dark-brown-painted wall that run the length of the venue. Fluorescent light panels in the wall emphasize perspective: an installation by English artist Louise Sudell, these mood-altering panels are programmed to change from warm red to turquoise blue. In the habitable areas Studiox applied a lighter palette described as a 'homage to the 1950s' with toffee brown, beige, pistachio, yellow and khaki.

A yellow sofa fabricated from high-density foam and finished with synthetic leather wraps around the walls defining the formal restaurant area. 'This was designed especially for the place, with an ergonomic chair-like shape for comfort,' says Rapelius. The dining chairs are designed by Maarten Van Severen and produced by Vitra. Stunning vintage 1950s white Murano glass pendant lamps give Lupino an injection of retro style: 'We found them in a flea market in Madrid; a hotel had thrown them out when it was being renovated.' The smaller matching table lamps were turned into wall lights for the casual dining area at the rear.

Opposite:
1950s Murano table lamps, salvaged from a flea market, illuminate the restaurant area.

Left:
Next to the bar, a mood-altering light installation by English artist Louise Sudell is programmed to change from warm red to turquoise blue.

Plan:
The 50 metre (164 foot) long site is narrow, measuring from 4 to 7 metres (13 to 23 feet) wide; the ceiling rises to include a mezzanine towards the rear.

Locanda Locatelli bears the hallmarks of a David Collins production: quiet luxury, discretion and an understated decadence

Opposite:
Traces of the refined glamour
of 1940s theatrical design
and Art Deco are visible in
Collins's restaurant interiors,
customized furniture
and lighting.

Right:
Convex mirrors, like reflective
portholes, possibly inspired
one critic's reference to
'ocean liner luxury'.

Far right:
Zebrano cladding enriches the
interior and adds a sense of
louche 1970s luxury.

Locanda Locatelli, London, UK
February 2002
David Collins

When London-based Italian chef Giorgio Locatelli opened Locanda Locatelli in early 2002 it was an overnight success and earned one Michelin star within its first year. It's no wonder that such a high-pedigree chef should commission London's most prolific restaurant designer, architect David Collins, to create his new eponymous restaurant.

Although Locanda Locatelli has its own distinctive identity, it bears the hallmarks of a David Collins production: quiet luxury, discretion and an understated decadence reminiscent of 1940s theatrical design and Art Deco. Locatelli says of their first meeting (*Observer*, 19 January 2003): 'David walked in, whistling, sat on a pile of wood, and said: "So, what do you want to cook here?" We talked till one in the morning. Someone had to go out and get a kebab for us. We're both Catholic boys. We've got this thing with our mothers. So it was always gonna be him, and I am so pleased with the result.'

Locanda Locatelli is located in the Churchill Intercontinental Hotel, but like all good destination hotel restaurants it has an independent street entrance. No structural changes were necessary to the 90-cover dining room, which measures 200 square metres (2,150 square feet). Collins has encapsulated the warmth and richness of Locatelli's Italian food through an earthy palette, amber lighting and the bold use of heavy-grain timber. Biscuit and caramel leather banquettes line the walls and large, hemispherical booth banquettes snake down the centre of the room, creating a fluid S-shape. These are paired with custom-made armchairs designed to swivel, to ease access and minimize noise. Acoustics are moderated further by the turquoise woven horsehair wall panelling, guaranteeing a clandestine hush. The internal support columns are the anchor and heart of the room, clad in zebrano-wood veneer to appear like staggered stacks of solid beams.

At a Michelin-rated level of dining, discretion is key. Glass screens featuring hand-painted iridescent golden strands afford an element of privacy. Along the rear wall a series of Art Deco-style convex mirrors reflect the room like fish-eye lenses. These reflective 'portholes' may have prompted a critic's reference to 'ocean liner luxury' when describing Locanda Locatelli.

A great believer in the flattering effects of indirect lighting, Collins always creates his own. Here, square lights fabricated from glass rods, hand-cast glass and parchment echo the geometry of the zebrano-clad columns. Spotlights illuminate linen-dressed tables and candlelight creates a romantic aura by night. Regular diners at Locanda Locatelli include British Prime Minister Tony Blair and his wife Cherie, and it is rumoured to be the 'local' Italian for Madonna and Guy Ritchie. Now that's star rating.

Diners travel through Comerç 24, guided by splashes of yellow and red offering 'pockets' of drinking and dining

Opposite:
The wine display is given
accents of colour, in keeping
with the rest of the interior.

Above left:
The view from the front of the
restaurant shows the yellow
bar stools to the right and the
dining area beyond.

Above centre:
A pocket of red, where guests
can rest en route to the
dining room.

Above right:
The rather sombre dining
room is 'bookended' by yellow
and red alcoves.

Comerç 24, Barcelona, Spain
June 2001
Xavier Abellàn, Anna Rius & Alfons Tost

The spirit of Mondrian lives on in the interior of
Barcelona's Comerç 24. Bold geometric blocks of primary
colour contrast with the older 19th-century stone
architecture, like a 3D incarnation of the artist's abstract
neo-plasticism compositions. Comerç 24 is located in
Barcelona's hip cultural hub, El Born. Compared to
London's 'Soho, Covent Garden and Notting Hill all rolled
into one', this small, funky neighbourhood in the old part
of the city buzzes with designer shops, art galleries and
clothing boutiques by day and hums with vibrant nightlife
after dark. Born is brimming with stylish restaurants, cool
cocktail lounges, wine bars and clubs attracting visitors
and locals alike.

Comerç 24 occupies the empty storehouse of
the old wholesale market, Mercat del Born, constructed
in 1870. Confronted with a difficult space, the team of
architects and designers decided to organize the internal
elements to create a journey: diners travel through the
otherwise neutral space enticed and guided by splashes
of yellow and red offering 'pockets' of drinking and dining.
Hence the orchestration of a loop that leads from the
entrance, winding past the show-kitchen to the dining
room located at the front of the property.

Adjacent to the entrance are a couple of dining
tables framed by shelving displaying wines. These are
brightened by accents of colour as clear bottles glow with
red and yellow uplighting. Beyond this is the bar area,
where yellow dominates: the long bar, set at a diagonal, is
flanked by high stools upholstered in bright yellow to match
the back bar.

At the rear of the space and at an oblique angle
are windows offering views of the kitchen, lined in
contrasting green tiles. There are two group tables in this
'kitchen-lobby' space. Opposite the bar, against the stone
wall, a backlit layer of yellow matt plastic forms a backdrop
to a table for six that appears to be cantilevered from the
kitchen. Directly opposite the kitchen is an oval table for
six, defined by five stone support columns and a red
ceiling panel mirroring the red upholstered furniture below.
En route to the dining room, a low bench-recliner and red
chair appear like sculptures against a landscape panel of
red plastic. Beech furniture has been stained wenge colour
throughout for consistency.

The dining room in contrast is sombre and
grey, but brightened by colourful 'bookends': at each end,
group tables sit in alcoves panelled in yellow and red
plastic with the accompanying long benches upholstered
to match. Aside from the two lighting installations
decoration is kept to a clean, modern minimum. Single
yellow and red roses in vases adorn tables and in one
slender dining alcove a giant monochrome portrait features
a praying man. The lighting is equally restrained: halogen
ceiling spots and recessed lighting are used to emphasize
pockets of colour or to guide the diner through the
'journey' that is Comerç 24.

Left:
Icebergs is totally in tune with its surroundings; the transparent glass balustrade allows the external and internal to blend seamlessly.

Above:
Turquoise blues and straw-hued loom chairs reflect the natural beach palette outside.

Icebergs, Sydney, Australia
December 2002
Lazzarini Pickering Architetti

Designing a restaurant in a city where what's on the outside often counts more than what's on the inside is perhaps daunting enough. Designing a restaurant in full view of the city's most famous outdoor 'postcard' destination could be very intimidating indeed. Not, however, if you're the Rome-based architects Lazzarini Pickering Architetti, who rose gallantly to the challenge of creating Bondi Icebergs' new restaurant and bar on a clifftop overlooking Sydney's Bondi Beach and the Pacific Ocean. No doubt it helps that one half of the duo, Australian Carl Pickering, is a native fully in tune with the city's beach culture. Their design is a serene, sophisticated response to the stunning natural scenery of Bondi – a name derived from the Aboriginal word Boondi which means 'water breaking over rocks'.

Icebergs' dining room and restaurant occupies the top floor of the Bondi Icebergs' winter swimming club, an Australian institution with a seawater pool that was established in 1929 and is famous for being the very first such club. These clubs are often the socializing nucleus of beach communities in Australia. Lazzarini Pickering's modern design has revived the slightly faded reputation of

Bondi Icebergs, described by one reviewer as 'Manhattan by way of the Aegean': the restaurant and bar is now one of Sydney's hippest destinations.

Lazzarini Pickering say of the project, undertaken in association with Tanner Associates, 'one has attempted to interpret one of Australia's most spectacular sites while also interpreting one of Australia's greatest restaurateurs, Maurice Terzini, famous for his intimate, welcoming spaces'. This combination, along with the domestic proportions of the 50 x 5 metre (160 x 16 foot) rectilinear space, inspired them to create 'the atmosphere of a beach house rather than a restaurant', a simple, almost self-effacing design that would maximize views and not detract from the stunning marine panorama.

Patrons enter a reception area defined by four circular chandelier screens. The 'geometrical heart of the project', this lobby divides the bar on the left from the 105-cover dining room on the right. Not only do these chandelier-screens filter the view of the two separate areas from new arrivals, but they also sway in the sea breeze like giant wind chimes. The washed-out beach colours of the fine, sand-like aggregate concrete floor and straw-hued loom chairs combine with watery blues to embody the natural, weather-worn nautical palette outside. 'The colours of the fabrics echo those of the pool and sea outside,' explain Lazzarini Pickering, 'from the turquoises and aquamarines of clear, sunny days to the dark greens and purples of grey, stormy afternoons.'

In the restaurant, glossy C-shaped, steel-framed aquamarine glass seating structures have been extended out onto the terrace to 'dilate the space'. Like crystallized waves or elongated sea loungers, these reproportion the long balcony while echoing the refreshing turquoise seawater pool below.

Contrasting materials were used to distinguish the lighter public spaces looking out to sea from staff and service elements along the street elevation. 'The body of the servant spaces is built in charcoal and black laminate and the dark tones of their interiors absorb the light so as not to interfere with the restaurant atmosphere every time a door is opened,' explain Lazzarini Pickering. Furthermore, the dark tones are 'a memory of Maurice Terzini's signature dark, intimate restaurants and they also prevent any reflections in the large glass windows at night, allowing a perfect view of the lit beach and pool over to north Bondi.'

The finishing touches are the huge, custom-designed chandeliers, measuring between 2.2 and 5 metres (7 and 16 feet) each. These bear free-moving faux-candle lamps activated by an electromagnetic impulse to keep the 'flames' realistically flickering every 20 seconds and set the restaurant and bar a-twinkle by night.

Icebergs

Stuttgart's Oggi is a Zen shrine to simplicity and clean lines

Opposite:
Toffee-coloured nutwood has
been used throughout to
counterbalance the vast glass
façade and add warmth.

Top right:
The more formal half of the
restaurant features classic
white linen.

Bottom right:
One of the angled inner walls
contains display niches,
brightened up here with
orange pumpkins.

Oggi, Stuttgart, Germany
December 2001
Lamott Architekten

Contemporary Italian restaurant Oggi (Today)
is a Zen shrine to simplicity and clean lines. Lamott
Architekten converted the former Mövenpick restaurant into
Oggi by applying the bare minimum in terms of materials
and palette. The 300 square metre (3,230 square foot)
restaurant occupies the ground floor of a bank designed
by the celebrated German architect Rolf Gutbrod; it is
located in the centre of Stuttgart, directly beside the major
Schlossplatz in an area that is becoming a restaurant and
bar hot spot.

Lamott answered the brief to create a
restaurant, bar and bistro through configuration of space.
The bar is at the heart of the space: crisp linen-dressed
tables define the restaurant on the left, and exposed timber
tables the bistro on the right. Clean lines dominate the
interior, which has been constructed using entirely natural
materials. Bright, natural light floods in from the large,
glazed frontage. The stark white walls and linen are
counterbalanced by the black basaltino stone floor and
bar façade and mid-brown hues of the nut-wood wall-
panelling, bar top and furniture. Toffee-hued nut-wood
was chosen specifically, as Angus Lamott explains,
'because we liked the contrast with the cool glass walls
and the black floor; we felt it introduces a warm
atmosphere to the room'.

The ground floor exterior juts out at an angle
from the main building; inside, staggered nut-wood-clad
façades conceal and unite three isolated existing irregular
inner walls. The purity of the interior architecture is
emphasized by lighting: simple strip lights integrated into
the suspended ceiling highlight perspective and enhance
the sense of space, while recessed lighting at the ceiling's
edge makes the inner facades of nut-wood more
prominent, counteracting the cooler light from the windows
opposite. Niches in the rear nut-wood wall house waiter
stations, bottles behind the bar and, in the restaurant,
seasonal vegetables (in the image on the right they are
pumpkins) to add a dash of colour.

By day Fritz Fischer operates as a work canteen, but during the evening it morphs into an upscale restaurant and cocktail lounge

Opposite:
The restaurant area with
the cocktail lounge beyond;
diaphanous white drapes
form moveable partitions
between areas.

Right:
The cocktail lounge is
differentiated from the
restaurant by its raised
height, different lighting
and low lounge furniture.

Far right:
The chunky bar consists of
a white laminate front and a
dark smoked oak counter

Fritz Fischer, Berlin, Germany
January 2003
Uli Lechtleitner

Fritz Fischer exemplifies the 'less is more' approach that appears to be so popular in modern German restaurant design. It is located on the bank of the River Spree in the ground floor of the German headquarters of Universal Music in Berlin, built in the 1920s as an egg storage warehouse. Recently refurbished to create the corporate office, the original brick façade is listed as a landmark. The distinctive property overlooks the river and surrounding stone warehouses, harbour quays and new office buildings in a lively neighbourhood on the border of Kreuzberg and Friedrichshain attracting young residents, bars, clubs and independent businesses.

Fritz Fischer leads a double life: by day it operates as the work canteen for Universal Music Group employees, but during the evening it morphs into a 100-cover 'upscale restaurant and cocktail lounge'. During spring and summer the large riverside terrace, complete with beer garden and barbecue grill, extends the capacity

by a further 70 seats. The layout has been designed to facilitate the dual function of lunchtime canteen and evening restaurant. During the day people enter from the ground-floor foyer of Universal Music, passing through the bar and coffee shop. The self-service counter is situated behind a fibreglass wall separating the kitchen and the free-flow area from the restaurant and lounge. Access is provided between the self-service and dining area through double doors, each 2 metres (6 feet 6 inches) wide, set into the fibreglass wall. In daytime the view takes precedence and the white-painted columns, walls and ceiling reflect the water outside: the surfaces of the columns are polished with wax to maximize the play of light.

In the evening the double doors are closed and the fibreglass wall illuminated to form a glowing backdrop for the restaurant. Diners arrive on the opposite side of the space, where the street entrance leads into a reception lobby, separated from the restaurant by diaphanous white drapes. These drapes are used throughout Fritz Fischer to make flexible distinctions between areas, for example between the dining area and the lounge, which is also raised slightly to enable a smooth division without

obstructing the flow of space. By night, simple cylindrical ceiling lights, fixed high above so as not to detract from the sense of space, radiate a warm, diffuse yellow light. In the lounge smaller pendant versions of the lights hang lower, compressing the space and making this area more intimate.

The pared-down linear aesthetic is reinforced by the dark smoked oak floor that runs throughout and the matching timber and white laminate furniture. Tables are hewn from dark smoked oak and have white laminate surfaces, and the lounge banquettes have smoked oak frames with white leather upholstered seats. In creating Fritz Fischer, Uli Lechtleitner takes 'simple' straight to the edge.

Fusion is a cool, understated alternative to the primary colours on display elsewhere in the hotel.

Fusion, Hamburg, Germany
April 2001
Matteo Thun Partners

Hamburg's Side Hotel has been a popular addition to the city's growing breed of hip hotels. It was created by architects William Alsop and Jan Störmer, with interior spaces by Milan-based designer and architect Matteo Thun. Situated in the centre of the city, close to the most exclusive shopping district and the opera house, it has been described as a 'chic hideaway'. Like many new boutique hotels, Side is not used purely by foreign visitors: local media professionals, fashionistas and style-savvy urbanites also frequent the Fusion restaurant and bar. Both are located on the ground floor and benefit from a separate street entrance. The bar is aligned with the front elevation and the restaurant lies perpendicular to it, stretching back along the side elevation of the hotel.

Compared with other public areas of Side, the restaurant and bar are probably its most classic spaces. Indeed Thun says, 'It is this area of the hotel that reflects the clean design, no-design in which regular clientele will feel comfortable passing time beyond that dedicated to consuming their meal – a space to be savoured slowly.' The clean lines, dark timber and stark white linen of the restaurant are a cool, understated alternative to the primary colours in the pool and spa area and of Thun's ovoid, Super Sassi furniture in the hotel lobby and reception. Diners are accommodated on white linen-covered 'soft' chairs, on leather benches or in the boxy armchairs of the sushi bar. A large, rectilinear ceiling insert sends out a diffuse light; by night, candles add atmosphere.

The neighbouring bar is somewhat brighter, with chunky red leather bar stools (called Toys 1) and low coffee-table seats (Toys 2) set against the wood-panelled room. Polished onyx tables incorporate mini gameboy-sized televisions playing calming videos of goldfish. A window onto the adjacent hotel lobby is lit by a row of candles, lending it the appearance of a hearth. The bold colours of the furniture are reflected in the reflective surfaces of the back bar, clad in satinated extra-white mirror.

Left:
Fusion offers a more classic experience, compared to the other, rather quirky, public areas of the hotel.

Below:
The adjacent bar is furnished with bright-red leather furniture and table-cum-televisions.

High Concept

Craft restaurant deconstructs, strips back and lays bare the 'art' of cooking and architecture

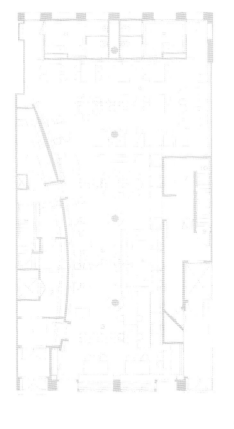

Craft, New York City, USA
March 2001
Bentel & Bentel Architects

Craft by name and craft by nature. Craft
restaurant, located in Manhattan's former 'Ladies' Mile'
shopping district, deconstructs, strips back and lays bare
the 'art' of cooking and architecture. Award-winning chef-
patron Tom Colicchio believes that cooking is a matter of
craftsmanship rather than art. His food concept for Craft
was, 'to explore the full flavour of each artisanally raised
ingredient on the seasonal menu, and serve these
unadorned on separate plates for all to share'. Impressed
by the honest simplicity of his vision, Bentel & Bentel
Architects were inspired to create an interior in keeping
with his philosophy. 'Our goal was to shape, within the
wreck of this former department store built in 1886, a
simple yet texturally and spatially rich interior that
integrates with the food and service both functionally
and metaphorically,' says Peter Bentel.

It is the rustic warmth of natural materials and
the contrast in textures that first alert the eye. Bentel &
Bentel have taken care to 'balance new construction
against existing, noble materials against plain'. The contrast
serves a purpose, as co-partner Paul Bentel explains: 'By
visual and tactile comparison of the materials that make up
each element the patron's sensual appreciation of those
materials deepens.' Hence the 'opposites attract'

aesthetic: the rough wood-fibre ceiling versus the rich, polished sheen of the Brazilian walnut (imbuia) floor below; the soft, sweeping arc of the leather-panelled wall accentuated by the cool, cage-like rigidity of the wine vault opposite. Existing elements include the raw-terracotta-block-clad columns and exposed brickwork, to which Bentel & Bentel have added clusters of naked Tesla lamps, or squirrel-bulbs, which highlight the original bones of the building.

To meet the client's practical requirements the scheme had to accommodate seating for 130 diners, a 3,500-bottle wine-storage facility, a 204 square metre (2,200 square foot) kitchen spread over a 276 square metre (2,975 square foot) ground floor, and a 228 square metre (2,450 square foot) cellar. This was achieved by placing the kitchen in the cellar and taking full advantage of the 4.3 metre (14 foot) high ground-floor space by constructing a two-storey wine vault along most of the east wall of the 24 metre (80 foot) long dining room. The wine wall not only conceals the service route from kitchen to dining room: it also creates a dramatic first impression as it is directly opposite the bronze-clad entrance.

Housed within this vast steel and bronze installation is the restaurant holding bar, flanked by 'Danko' cherry plywood bar stools, tailor-modified for the project. The bar top, a centimetre (½ inch) thick slab of steel, epitomizes Bentel & Bentel's approach, that the restaurant should have well-crafted items, but also items directly involved in the making of the restaurant. Peter Bentel explains, 'The bar top is the actual steel top from the work table in the ironmonger's studio that was used to make the wine wall and bar. There is a patina of age (the steel is waxed and has been allowed to oxidize slightly) and also a patina of work – we hope that the "auratic presence" of the craftspeople who made the wine wall is felt by those who sit at the bar.' There are few secrets here – even the leather-panelled wall opposite bears its construction stitches with pride.

At the rear of the restaurant the expanse of space is enhanced by an abstract blue triptych stretching across the end wall like a panoramic distant horizon. Adjoining this, recessed lighting illuminates the original brick wall, adding a sense of depth. Custom-made cherrywood dining tables include a nifty drawer detail for storing wine-related accessories. These drawers also function as bases for extension leaves to increase the number of possible seats at any one table. The craftsmanship of every individual component of Craft may be admired in isolation, but the components also work together as an absorbing whole.

Left:
The nuts, bolts and stitching of the leather-panelled wall, shown in close-up.

Far left:
Two decks of glass-fronted cabinets reveal dozens of wine bottles, each lying in its own steel mesh hammock.

Right:
Banquette seating lines the exposed-brick wall at the rear, increasing the number of covers.

Opium's white fractal form envelops the dining room like a frozen tidal wave

Opposite:
Misho and Kiechle's
sculpture embraces the
space, while also functioning
as an extremely effective
acoustic backdrop.

Far right:
View of the white cardboard
construction from the
mezzanine cocktail lounge.

Sketch:
Sculptor Kiechle found
inspiration in the city, where
people love natural and
organic shapes: 'They love
the Opera House. They are
drawn to the water and the
Botanical Gardens.'

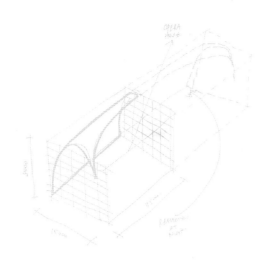

Opium, Sydney, Australia
December 2001
Misho + Associates

In 2001 the former Sydney Cove International Passenger Terminal on the Circular Quay foreshore, close to the Museum of Modern Art, was redeveloped to accommodate a string of new destination restaurants, of which one was Opium. Although the location was prime, with fantastic views of the Opera House across the water, the original owner and veteran restaurateur Wolfie Pizem recognized that the sheer size of the space was problematic and that as a restaurant it would lack intimacy. He commissioned Misho + Associates to 'transform the double-height space into an intimate hub targeted at the supper set'.

Architect and interior designer Misho explains: 'The space is really deep, industrial and very intimidating as a restaurant, it was too big and needed compression.' However, there were building restrictions; the Department of Public Works stipulated that the view from Circular Quay West through the restaurant to the Opera House must not be obscured. Misho + Associates solved part of this problem by inserting a new cantilevered mezzanine, like many neighbouring venues along the same stretch, creating a cosy cocktail lounge overlooking the restaurant.

But the real tour de force of Opium is the white fractal form that wraps up and over the dining room like a frozen tidal wave. Misho's initial concept focused on a curved organic structure as a way 'to pull back the space, add interest and create warmth'. Midway through the project the budget was slashed from 2.5 to 1.5 million Australian dollars (US$1.6 to $1 million) and his idea seemed increasingly impossible to realize. Fortunately, Misho was introduced to Horst Kiechle, an engineer turned sculptor, and together they worked on a solution.

Misho's initial concept was developed using Kiechle's high-tech art computer programme: the pair developed the vast, sweeping wave with the aid of a geometric equation comprising 4,500 unique cutting patterns – like Origami on a dramatic scale. It was constructed using laminated white (fire-rated) cardboard panels, as Misho explains: 'Restaurants are faddy, food changes according to fashion and chefs are extremely transient; they're not about longevity. So if a restaurant is going to survive – because we all want something different constantly and we get bored with going to the same place – the idea was that the whole ceiling could change. It could be pulled down, recycled and replaced by a new organic shape, maybe in a different colour.'

There was no deliberate attempt to model the sculpture on the Opera House, although as Misho says, 'The sculpture establishes a relationship with the Opera House through its expressive and organic form, framing the spectacular views of Sydney Cove'.

The remainder of the restaurant is simple and low key with dark, polished timber floors, earthy brown wicker furniture, a few occasional lamps and tables lit by candlelight. This provides a solid, grounded environment to compliment the fluidity of the installation, which is glamorously uplit by night.

In 2003 the restaurant, originally called Bambu, was bought by Tonci Farac – owner of the adjacent Wildfire – and given its current name, Opium.

Khoury says 'Centrale tries to escape that typical process of construction by re-enacting traditional ways of making.'

Top left:
Adjoining the 'general assembly' dining room is a smaller dining annexe, which contains three separate loggias, each seating six diners.

Bottom left:
This aerial view shows the floodlit rear of the site, below which Khoury has placed the underground kitchen.

Far left:
Centrale's crumbling façade is encased in a metal mesh to 'enhance the poetic dimension of decay.'

Below:
The diners' view of the bar underbelly, illuminated by a large, utilitarian light fixture.

Centrale, Beirut, Lebanon
September 2001
Bernard Khoury Architects

Lebanese architect Bernard Khoury is a man with a mission. A Beirut native, he is passionately dedicated to the recuperation of his war-ravaged city, which was quite literally torn in half during the 1975–91 conflict. He not only works practically to restore damaged buildings, but also champions the 'progressive mutation of war-damaged buildings in Beirut'. In 2001 his work earned him a nomination for the municipality of Rome's prestigious international Premio Borromini Award for young architects. Khoury's intention is to confront what he calls the 'collective amnesia' about the war years through renovation and rebuilding. Although his unusual projects, like B018 and Centrale, appear to rise, Phoenix-like from the ashes and ruins of the city, they are often brutal statements and visual reminders of Beirut's horrific past.

Centrale occupies a 1920s residential building in Nasra, an area that was a deserted no man's land during the war due to its proximity to the demarcation line dividing Beirut. Nasra is on the periphery of the Beirut Central District, an area which has been inhabited for 5,000 years and is full of historically classified buildings and currently undergoing rigorous redevelopment. The past decade has seen extensive construction in Beirut, although many argue that there is 'contempt for conservation'. Since land is

valuable and restoration expensive, there has been substantial demolition as opposed to sensitive restoration. This makes French restaurant and bar Centrale all the more impressive, with its brave juxtaposition and adaptation of industrial, rehabilitated materials with an old, decaying shell.

Khoury has deliberately applied low-tech building techniques here: 'The Centrale project tries to escape that typical process of construction by re-enacting traditional ways of making'. All the steel elements were assembled on site in a continuous weld technique. Initially the derelict building's unsafe internal walls and first floor were demolished, which left a 9 metre (30 foot) high space. In the process, reinforcement was necessary: 'Horizontal beams were used to embrace the skin from the outer perimeter of the façade, while an internal structural layer of concrete was poured against the internal surface of the envelope'. Ring beams spanning the whole width of the space were used to brace the walls from the inside. These are traditionally a temporary part of the process, but Khoury has retained the four ring beams to dramatic effect: 'They now imply a new reading of the non-restored façade,' he says.

The crumbling sandstone façade has not been replastered and restored to its former glory. Instead, it is veiled by a metallic mesh and protected by a waterproofing membrane applied between the sandstone and the internal layer of concrete. As Khoury explains, 'The mesh now enhances the poetic dimension of decay. That explains the nature of the intervention, its temporal dimension and its position vis-à-vis the "historical value" of the building.'

Inside, the restaurant occupies the double-height space beneath the belly of the bar. Reminiscent of a formal war cabinet or general assembly conference room, the black-stained mahogany table seats 46 diners. Service routes are 'trapped inside the table' and lead down a flight of stairs to the underground kitchen, which is located beneath the garden area outside. Individual pilot lamps illuminate each place setting, and the timber wall slats (blocking windows) and high-backed leather chairs 'ensure the secrecy of the assembly'. A large, utilitarian light fixture illuminates the bracing structure, the bar underbelly ten metres above. Paved concrete provides durable flooring and connects Centrale to the raw urban context outside.

Patrons reach the rooftop bar via an elevator, which houses two facing benches and is the mobile end-section of the cylindrical volume of the bar. Four ring beams describe a circular section occupied by a 17 metre (56 foot) long dark-stained mahogany bar. This tubular dome thus appears to emerge from the roof of a disintegrating ruin, like a glowing skyline bunker in reverse. The pièce de résistance (like that of B018) is the retractable roof, affording guests a drink beneath the stars. As the maverick Khoury explains, 'The ring beam structure serves as a track for the rotating movement of the cylindrical envelope of the bar. When open, it frames a view of the city: a juxtaposition of renovated edifices and a non-renovated fabric at the edge.' If Khoury succeeds, Beirut's recuperation will be an uplifting trajectory, a city elevating itself from the debris and looking to the stars.

Below left:
From above, the tubular rooftop bar suggests an almost alien provenance.

Model:
This cross-section computer model shows the bar, with the dining room below and stairs down to the underground kitchen, connected by an elevator at one end.

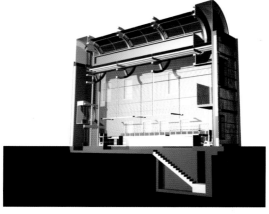

Below:
Centrale's bar features a
retractable roof, allowing
guests the experience of
drinking beneath the stars.

Every cloud has a silver
lining at **Georges**, the sky-high Costes Brothers
restaurant atop the Pompidou Centre

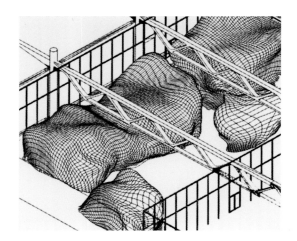

Left:
The 'blobular' form housing
the video room is lined with
yellow rubber and covered
with brushed aluminium.
Tables are set in the open
space around it.

Plan:
A computer rendering shows
the arrangement of the four
blobular shells within the
existing hi-tech grid. Each
shell performs a specific
function: top left houses the
kitchen, top right the VIP
room, bottom right the video
room and bottom left the
coat check.

Georges, Paris, France
February 2000
Jakob + MacFarlane

You could say that every cloud has a silver lining
at Georges, the sky-high Costes Brothers restaurant on the
fifth floor of the hi-tech Georges Pompidou Centre in Paris.
Innovative architectural duo Dominique Jakob and Brendan
MacFarlane wanted to create a 'floating sensation in
relation to the city', hence the silver sculptures redolent of
an organic cloud formation, hovering, trapped inside the
industrial grid of Renzo Piano and Richard Rogers's hi-tech
masterpiece.

It was the host building and the incredible views
of the Paris skyline that inspired Jakob and MacFarlane:
'It was how to work around these and create something
from this, to form a dialogue with the structure but then
produce something unexpected.' The amorphous silver
shapes appear almost inflatable, rising up towards the
blue and silver ductwork 9 metres (30 feet) above, but
melting and deforming in other areas to accommodate
major structural beams. Reminiscent of Frank Gehry's
work, the sculpted aluminium shells have been variously
described as aortic valves, clouds and grottos, and by
their creators as pockets of space.

Diners approach Georges from a terrace, seating 150 diners during summer and affording fantastic views of Paris and the internal geography of the restaurant, reflected in a Zen-like rooftop pool. The shells appear like outer-space caves transported from a distant planet, forming a futuristic landscape in the glass-enclosed 900 square metre (9,700 square foot) interior. All reveal colourful vinyl linings, coded for different functions. The largest shell, with a grey interior, houses the kitchen; the restrooms and cloakroom inhabit the lime-green shell; the bar is cocooned in the yellow shell; and the red shell, which can be closed entirely, is the VIP dining lounge.

Georges accommodates up to 200 diners at tables adhering to a strict grid arrangement dictated by the large aluminium floor tiles. Opaque glass-topped tables are flanked by low, broad-backed white chairs, designed by Jakob + MacFarlane. After dark, waiters activate an internal spotlight on each table with a toothpick, illuminating the slender glass vases containing single-stem roses or tulips. This central table light is essential for diners wanting to discover the cost of their Parisian-Asian meal. The menus consist of sheer ivory paper, the prices written backwards on the reverse of the side listing the dishes: shed backlighting on the matter, and all is revealed. But there is plenty in the breathtaking views of Paris and shapely interior terrain to distract diners from such details.

Nectar strikes a distinctive, playful pose at the Bellagio, Las Vegas

Nectar, Las Vegas, USA
September 2001
Jordan Mozer & Associates

As an architect or designer, where better to let your imagination run riot than Las Vegas, a flashy, neon city founded on fantasy? This adult playground of artifice is the ideal environment for wild creations. Chicago-based designer Jordan Mozer leapt to the rescue when Sam's American Grill, one of numerous restaurant and bar concessions in the vast Bellagio Hotel and Casino resort, required a complete renovation. He transformed the existing restaurant into the quirky, whimsical Nectar – named after the food of the gods.

Located at the entrance of the Bellagio retail corridor, Nectar strikes a distinctive, playful pose: curvaceous white columns rise up to support a lattice of beams forming the restaurant ceiling. The beams 'were inspired by the use of trees as columns in indigenous architecture in the south-western United States,' explains Mozer: 'beams would frame … the columns at the place where trees branched; this was a naturally strong cradle for the beams.'

Overseen by chef John Schenk, the 136-cover restaurant offers contemporary American food, while the small adjoining bar serves seafood and oysters. 'The idea of the primitive architecture is in keeping with the philosophy of the food,' says Mozer: 'it's back to basics, there are lots of grilled fish and meat dishes, most of which are cooked with organic (wood-burning) fuels. So I designed the restaurant with warm, earthy colours to reflect this cooking.'

The bone-like columns are highlighted against richly textured walls of patinated copper and bespoke furnishings: burgundy mohair banquettes and chairs with cream leather seats. Mozer's autumnal palette of tawny, natural tones creates a warm, inviting interior. The open kitchen gives added drama, organized as it is for maximum showcase effect with a wood-burning grill as 'the kitchen's signature piece' in the foreground, affording diners clear views of the chefs at work.

The tree theme is repeated throughout the scheme in the busy, 1960s psychedelic-style carpet, the cast magnesium aluminium twiggy frames of the dining chairs and the metal branch-like lamps with hand-blown glass shades.

The soft, sculpted column motif of the restaurant is carried through to the funky, futuristic 33-seat bar, described as a 'pastel-coloured cool oasis', the cool polar opposite to the warm, rustic restaurant. 'Las Vegas is really hot and it's a dry heat,' says Mozer, 'so in the bar I wanted to emulate melted ice and a cooling atmosphere as opposed to the "cooked" restaurant interior.' Reminiscent of a space-ship capsule, the bar is a white glowing pod of fluid, 'melting' forms and smooth, polished surfaces, all contributing to the 'liquid cool' aesthetic. Shiny white stools complete the icy, futuristic look. A floor of epoxy-based terrazzo with blue glass chunks set into it curves up to form the bar and wraps around the base of a large central column. This centrepiece rises up to form a glowing, mushroom-like awning above the bar.

Whereas the restaurant is designed for relaxed dining, the bar is a far more stimulating space and acoustically louder. This was intentional, since it forms the transition point between the casino and the exclusive designer retail corridor housing big brands like Gucci, Prada, Armani and Chanel. High rollers and big spenders are no doubt detained en route to their retail therapy by this striking, ice-cool haven, since the barrier of funky silver railings in cast magnesium aluminium allows an unobstructed view of the bar.

Yabani attempts to describe a fraction of a society living in marvellous denial; it is not a 'postcard' building

Left:
Thirty-one 'ringside' seats
surround the sushi bar,
which in turn encircles
the transparent entrance/
exit shaft.

Above:
View through one of the glass
skylights to the shaft above.

Yabani, Beirut, Lebanon
March 2002
Bernard Khoury Architects

'Yabani attempts to describe a fraction of a
society living in marvellous denial,' explains Lebanese
architect Bernard Khoury of the Japanese restaurant
and bar in Beirut, 'it is not a "postcard" building, its
architecture attempts to reflect another urban reality.'
Khoury is a pioneering architect, playing an active role in
the recuperation and renovation of Beirut's architectural
casualties of war. Yabani (Lebanese for Japan) stands
proudly against an inhabited ruin, at the corner of
Damascus Road on the former demarcation line that
separated east and west Beirut during the 1975–91
conflict. Many of the surrounding buildings in the Nasra
area remain devastated, bullet-ridden and visibly scarred
by the war, but despite this some are refugee squats.

Yabani lies just a few metres from Monot Street,
where many bars and clubs have opened in recent years.
Indeed, Khoury calls it a 'monument for the entertainment
industry', commenting: 'Leftovers of war and spectacles
of desolation become a backdrop to the more impressive
spectacle of a society being entertained.' Placing the bold,
futuristic structure containing an underground restaurant,
bar and music club in such a bleak landscape has made
Yabani symbolic of wider issues. Khoury views post-war
Beirut as a 'hyper-contemporary version of the capitalist

city in a state of anarchy'. He presents Yabani as 'a bi-product of the environment through which it exists, a reinterpretation of magnified contradictions that are inherent in the present context'.

The glinting silver, steel and glass construction occupies a vacant lot: it was erected in six months and cost just under $800,000. Khoury excavated beneath the lot to create the subterranean two-storey concrete structure; this extends 14 metres (46 feet) above street level in the form of an aluminium-clad steel tower. Yabani sits on a circular base, or 'horizontal façade', flanked by panels of metal grating and defined by a timber perimeter and semicircular inner ring of horizontal glass 'walk-on' skylights. These provide natural light and sky views for diners in the restaurant on level -1 below. The ground level entrance is housed in a 7 metre (23 foot) high curved glass central opening or 'vitrine'. A receptionist welcomes patrons into a circular reception lobby activated by a hydraulic system, so it operates like a glass elevator and descends vertically to the restaurant or music club below.

Making an entrance is all part of the plan at Yabani, as Khoury stresses: 'Arrival and departure is intentionally overexposed as the reception lounge becomes the focal point around which the seating plan is generated'. Encircling the transparent mobile entrance/exit is a sushi bar with 31 ringside seats, custom-made for Yabani in mahogany and leather. The restaurant accommodates 85 diners in total: behind the first ring of seating is a passage leading to another ring of modular seating. These rings have fixed bases with modular tables facing a banquette that wraps around the perimeter of the circular wall.

There are two sunken 'Japanese' gardens located on either side of the circular plan, at the edges of the restaurant. Further seating in the form of four 'loggias', each accommodating six people, lines the perimeter of these gardens. The restaurant receives plenty of daylight from the ring of skylights above, and light filters down from the metal gratings directly above the sunken gardens. By night, additional illumination is provided by steel fixtures suspended from the ceiling, hovering like mechanical arms to spotlight the circular counter below. Beneath the restaurant are the Y'bar music club and lounge bar.

As Khoury points out, 'Patrons can enjoy their dining experience in total denial of the immediate urban surroundings … on the other hand, Yabani assumes its absurd presence and its impossible relationship with its urban environment through the exposure of the highly visible tower.' Yet again, Khoury has succeeded in creating post-apocalyptic architecture loaded with meanings: mindful of Beirut's past, commenting on its present and – by its very existence – a toast to its future.

Spanish architects RCR have blurred the boundaries between inside and out with their renovation of **Les Cols**

Left:
The long, refectory-style table
is flanked by walls of twisted,
golden metal that radiate a
fiery glow.

Les Cols, Olot City, Spain
June 2002
RCR Arquitectos

Spanish architects RCR have blurred the boundaries between inside and out with their renovation of Les Cols restaurant in Olot City. The pared-down palette of glass and steel, monastic simplicity and open-plan layout encourage interplay between the external space and the interior, maintaining a flow of light and views – Les Cols is situated in Catalonia's mountainous region of Garrotxa, renown for its volcanoes and outstanding natural beauty. The concept behind Les Cols is intrinsically linked to the soil on which it stands: its name is Catalan for 'the Cauliflowers'.

The restaurant occupies the ground floor of a grand old 13th-country house and is surrounded by lush foliage and vegetation. Self-subsistence is an integral element: the grounds of the house include a vegetable patch, a herb garden and free-range chickens. RCR were asked to enlarge the kitchen and enhance the link between the growing of produce and the cooking process. A porch extension was constructed around the perimeter of the original building to fulfil the brief.

There are three main areas: the new enlarged stainless steel kitchen, the main dining room and the gold salon; all are exposed to greenery or to the surrounding rural landscape. Natural light floods into the kitchen through floor-to-ceiling glazing which looks out onto a square outdoor patio. A neat hedge shields the kitchen patio from the entrance porch, where a '*lamina de agua*' (film of water) reflects the shubbery and kitchen beyond.

The sparseness of the 40-cover dining room, with its dark timber floors, is brightened by the custom-made golden steel furniture. Spartan, almost ecclesiastical in its aesthetic, the calm, rustic simplicity of the interior allows the food and the surrounding landscape to take precedence. A series of black steel screens, perpendicular to the floor-to-ceiling windows, lends the garden-side tables an air of intimacy. In summer the windows slide back and the dining room is open to the elements: as they say at Les Cols, 'Eating in the porch you are surrounded by open air, plants, aromas, and wonderful sights without missing the mysterious feel that these thick walls hold'.

By far the most impressive feature is the majestic gold salon. This accommodates 50 diners along one banquette table flanked by shimmering screens fabricated from twisted golden strands of steel. Open-ended, the room is accessible from the main restaurant entrance and looks out on to the pastoral scenery. Three adjoining private dining rooms, separated by the screens, benefit from the warm luminescence of this glowing room.

When it comes to 'location, location, location', Hamburg's **Herzblut** is definitely a local restaurant

Left:
Mozer used dark woods, earthy tones and low lighting for his reinvention of the traditional German tavern.

Right:
The hearts and anchor motif is reiterated throughout, for example in the form of the aluminium sculptures shown here.

Herzblut, Hamburg, Germany
March 2002
Jordan Mozer & Associates

When it comes to 'location, location, location', Hamburg's Herzblut is definitely a local restaurant. The logo of this former gambling hall, two intertwined red hearts pierced by an anchor and chain, represents the interests of the main client, the Holstein brewery, and is also highly symbolic of its location. It is situated on the Reeperbahn, a pulsating, mile-long artery in the heart of St Pauli (popularly known as '*der kietz*'), Hamburg's red light district. 'This is the wilder part of Hamburg,' explains designer Jordan Mozer, 'the Reeperbahn has been an entertainment district for many years because one of the largest harbours in Europe is at the end of it, so it's where all the sailors, pirates and whores have traditionally hung out.' However, that's not the only reason for the anchor and hearts. The Chicago-based firm Jordan Mozer & Associates designed Herzblut as a marketing vehicle for Holstein's Astra beer, a 'working-class' beer produced in the St Pauli neighbourhood, which bears a simplified logo of a heart containing an anchor.

Herzblut was conceived as a party destination for fans of the local football team, FC St Pauli, sponsored by Astra beer and also partners in the enterprise. It was FC St Pauli who inspired the name Herzblut: 'Literally translated it means heartblood, but it really means passion,' explains Mozer; 'the football club has an incredible following; everybody loves them because they're always the underdogs, but they have a lot of Herzblut.' Whilst working on the project Mozer watched them play against Munich and win, 'They sweated and struggled but in the end Herzblut won'.

Mozer describes the significance of the structural motif of swaying arches: 'FC St Pauli wear brown and white striped jerseys so the arches are wearing Italian glass mosaic stripes, and they're also dancing like they're playing ball.' The curvaceous forms, combined with the candlelit tables and earthy palette, certainly make Herzblut warm and inviting. Seating for 190 diners is arranged in simple, tavern-style rows towards the centre of the space, and bench-booths line two of the walls. These can be made more intimate by drawing across curtains, suspended from the ceiling between each booth; these also serve to reduce sound volumes.

The restaurant's design is based on an old tavern, as Mozer explains: 'We wanted to create a special tavern, so we've used a lot of classic dark wood. We wanted people to feel at home when they arrive, but then become amazed and surprised at the details, all of which are custom-made for the project.' Eye-catching details include the ceiling lighting, which exudes an organic charisma. The custom-made 'life lamps' comprise a copper hemisphere from which dangle hand-blown glass tentacles: 'They produce light like when sperm fuses with the egg', explains self-confessed idiosyncratic designer Mozer.

Other customized design highlights include the curvy velvet dining chairs and the colourful, Mondrian-style glass window separating the dining room from the open kitchen. This was both a design statement and an essential feature required by German law to provide natural daylight for the catering staff. Herzblut is described as an 'upscale casual' dining experience, something common in the USA but fairly experimental in Germany: 'The idea behind it is that the customers don't have to dress up to have a well-appointed, designed room', says Mozer. So far, the Herzblut is still winning.

Blue Fin glows brightly by night, like a glassy, Modernist box on the corner of Broadway

Left:
The candlelit *salon privé* on the second floor, with red-tinted, antique mirrored panelling.

Right:
In the bar, guests can knock back a cocktail while observing the neon blur of Times Square.

Blue Fin, New York, USA
December 2002
Yabu Pushelberg

Blue Fin glows brightly by night, like a glassy, Modernist box on the corner of Broadway in Manhattan's spruced-up Times Square. The seafood restaurant and bar are attached to the W New York Times Square Hotel, the 'designer label' of Starwood Hotels and Resorts, also designed by Yabu Pushelberg. Since forming their company in 1980, George Yabu and Glenn Pushelberg have created interiors for major international players, including Four Seasons Hotels & Resorts, Tiffany & Co. and The Grand Hyatt International. Their design philosophy? 'To reduce design to a number of powerful ideas: discreetly modern. More geared to the essence and quality of tranquillity. We seek to evoke feeling and visual emotion without an excess of design.'

As is often the case in Manhattan, the bar is the beacon for the restaurant: here that description is quite literal. Internally illuminated resin pedestals (aka drinking tables) are designed to lure customers inside. Described in *Interior Design* (September 2002) as 'Zen meets industrial chic', the bar is certainly pared down to a clean, almost futuristic white minimum. A terrazzo and marble floor offers a chic contrast to the gum-trodden concrete pavement outside.

Satin-finished stainless steel stools upholstered in white leather provide seating and the bar, lit from within, displays small white pebbles embedded in the resin façade.

Stepping from the bar into the restaurant behind, a liberal use of walnut timber on the floor, support columns and the 'Verso' dining tables make for a more classic environment. Blue Fin accommodates 400 diners over two levels connected by a sleek white staircase with a glass balustrade. This dramatic structural feature is set against a double-height, bas relief 'wave wall', the perfect backdrop for Japanese artist Hirotoshi Sawada's polycarbonate fish sculpture, suspended like a mobile and swimming in the same direction as the stairs. As Pushelberg says, 'The staircase is sculptural, beautiful and engaging, but in a very quiet way' (*Interior Design*, September 2002).

The exposed, double-height staircase lends the ground-floor dining room an airy, open feel, as does the backlit geometric mirror panelling lining the opposite wall. Cream booths and clusters of bright white lamps maintain a bright and refreshing look. Glenn Pushelberg describes it as 'fast, clattery and café-like' – albeit quite a luxurious café, with its white vinyl Saarinen chairs and warm timber. Tucked beneath the staircase is a sushi bar with a cast-concrete top and white pebble front. This below-stairs area is enlivened by backlit wall niches housing colourful Dinosaur Design tableware.

Left:
The bas-relief wall and Hirotoshi Sawada's fish sculpture lead the eye into the space.

Top left:
Mirrored panelling enhances the airy, open feel of the ground-floor dining area.

Plan:
Blue Fin occupies two levels in the corner of the W New York Times Square Hotel, which was also designed by Yabu Pushelberg.

Right:
Support beams were added to give the staircase a clean, cantilevered appearance.

Upstairs the atmosphere is far more intimate, with rich, natural textures, 'sensual finishes that invite people to relax and linger', says Pushelberg. Timber screens separate the main dining area from the bar, giving a sense of privacy but allowing glimpses between areas. A cosy, clubby aesthetic is achieved in the main dining room, with dark leather banquettes set into Deco-style recessed booths lined with aniline-dyed cowhide. The walls between the booths are clad in smoky, distressed antique mirror panelling.

There are several private dining rooms, the smallest of which is particularly spectacular. The walls of this moody den are wrapped in distressed red-tinted antique mirror panelling, with narrow walnut ledges supporting flickering candles. Diners are enveloped in a dusky red setting that magically twinkles as the mirrors reflect the flames into infinity.

Elsewhere in the main restaurant and private dining room, lighting is more of a statement: long lanterns constructed from hemp-wrapped wire frames, likened to 'lobster cages' or canoes, send out a textured amber glow.

Left:
Hemp-wrapped wire frames, reminiscent of lobster cages, house lights.

Below:
Timber slats, fixed to vertical rods, allow glimpses between the dining area and bar.

Morimoto offers

diners the sensation of floating in a cloud as it
drifts through a rainbow

Left:
View of the rainbow-coloured
dining room from the
mezzanine floor bar, framed
by bamboo lining.

Plan and section:
Three-dimensional renderings
show Rashid's organization
of the awkward 650 square
metre (7,000 square feet) space.

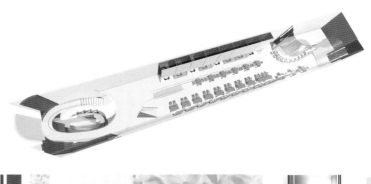

Morimoto, Philadelphia, USA
November 2002
Karim Rashid

Trailblazing restaurateur Stephen Starr strikes
again with his modern Japanese restaurant Morimoto.
Ever the design patron, this time he commissioned
'sensual minimalist' Karim Rashid to create the $1.5 million
interior. 'I saw Rashid as a brilliant product designer who
would bring a fresh approach to interior design, and I
discovered that he had a tremendous sensibility for Japan,'
he explains. 'I didn't want a traditional Japanese restaurant,
but rather the kind of cutting-edge space a designer might
create in Roppongi. I was looking for a place that was as
daring as Karim could make it, but warm.' (Frame no. 26,
May/June 2002). The result is quite ethereal. Philadelphia's
Morimoto appears almost gravity-defying, offering diners
the sensation of floating in a cloud (with silver lining) as it
drifts through a rainbow.

The eponymous hero is celebrity chef Masaharu
Morimoto, who rose to fame in the US as the star of a
cult TV show, the Japanese-produced Iron Chef. He
requested only two things: to be seen 'on stage', and for
everything in the bathrooms to be fully automatic. Rashid
was happy to comply: 'I feel very comfortable with both
issues because I understand "performance" and my own
home bathrooms are automatic. I love sensor technology
and all technologies that remove everyday banalities from

our lives.' Above and beyond these practicalities, Rashid consciously modelled the interior to complement Morimoto's cuisine. 'I think the contrast of the "raw" natural materials with the technology of LEDs was a perfect balance for the "raw" fusion style cooking.'

Rashid deliberately chose the more awkward site from two potential locations, as it 'forces you to be creative' (*Architectural Record* no.11, 2002). Deep and narrow, the 650 square metre (7,000 square foot) space is 73 metres (240 feet) long, 6.5 metres (21 feet) wide and 6 metres (19 feet) high. 'I wanted to make a long Cartesian grid of booths juxtaposed with a fluid organic space,' he explains. 'The bamboo ceiling and floor become one undulating organic envelope that starts out very low in the entrance – symbolic of bowing in traditional Japanese restaurants – to cleanse and prepare oneself for dining.' In the entrance foyer patrons are greeted by a large screen featuring a 3D winking Japanese girl and a shiny, black fibreglass sculpture by Rashid. Behind the screen a staircase leads up to the mezzanine bar, where drinkers can survey the glowing dining room below through a characteristically curvy 'blobist' window. Morimoto's stage is the bright yellow glass sushi bar at the opposite end of the restaurant.

The biomorphic curves of the bas-relief plasterwork (Japanese semi-gloss stucco over metal lathe) lend a fantastical feel, but it's the magical application of light that really breathes life into the scheme. The geometric central grid of seating booths and partitions dividing the wallside tables for two are constructed from hollow, frosted 15 centimetre (6 inch) wide glass boxes inside which LEDs are recessed into the floor at 1 centimetre (½ inch) intervals. These are programmed to gradually fade between four different colours, changing completely every 15 minutes. 'The colours speak of four moods, relaxation (aperitif – lilac), love (romantic – pink), conversation (energy – orange) and taste (flavour – green),' says Rashid. The subtlety is important: the new colour slowly washes through the space, drenching the cream walls and custom-designed cream leather seats in pastel hues without distracting diners from the food. In Rashid's words: 'The restaurant is much more flexible with the use of light. Light is the best architectural element because it is immaterial and therefore can transform a space completely; you feel like you are in a supernova, in another soft, organic dream-like world.'

Left:
Rashid's shiny, black organic sculpture in the entrance foyer, with winking girl behind.

Sketch:
An early sketch illustrates Rashid's organic approach to design.

Opposite:
Side tables, with the silver plaster wall behind.

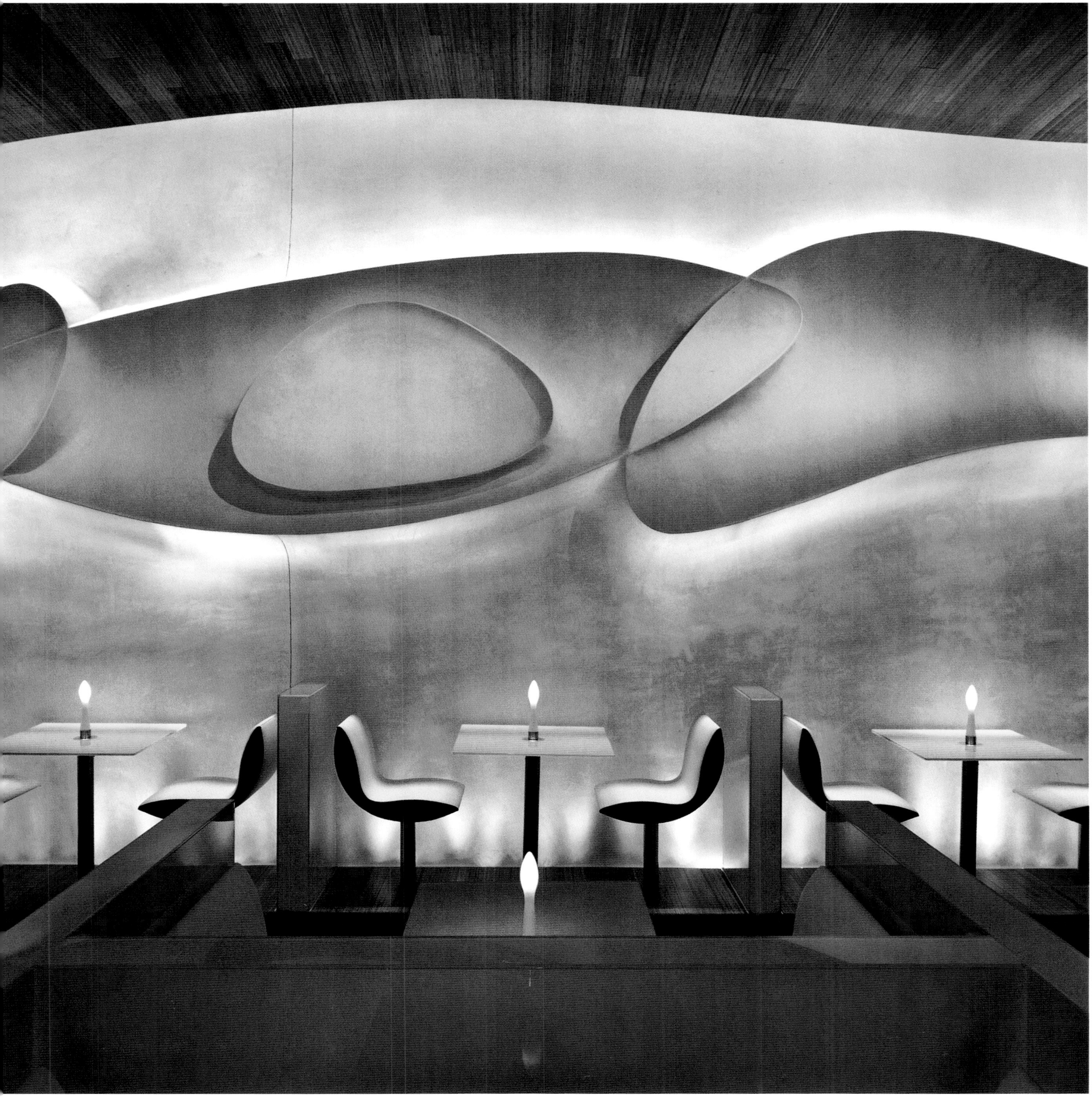

Cafeteria's designers have met the challenge of a large, windowless space by creating a spectacular interior landscape

Left:
Benchmark created the central installation according to Wells Mackereth's specifications, ensuring the correct footprint and height as well as the inclusion of a waiter station at one end, a long banquette and a group table at the other end.

Cafeteria, London, UK
May 2003
Wells Mackereth & Benchmark

Chef-proprietor John Torode and his partner Simon Wright discovered that inheriting a restaurant site can be a mixed blessing when they took over a building formerly occupied by Belgo in London's Ladbroke Grove. The cavernous, windowless space – designed by Foreign Office Architects in 1998 – originally cost around £2 million ($3 million) and as a consequence had good services. On a tight £200,000 ($300,000) budget Torode managed to transform the mollusc-inspired space into a brand new restaurant called Cafeteria. Inspired by its open-all-hours namesake in New York's Chelsea district, the UK Cafeteria is open for breakfast, lunch and dinner. To achieve his vision Torode appointed architects Wells Mackereth and the furniture design specialists Benchmark.

Cosmetic alterations included restaining the yellow oak of the interior skin to a darker, natural tone and giving the façade a facelift. Pink neon signage redolent of an American roadside diner elevates Cafeteria's street presence, and double-height glass-fronted doors were installed to further this effect.

The real challenge lay inside. 'We had to create an internal landscape to break up and fill the volume but also inject some kind of theatre inside,' says architect James Wells. Torode agreed – he was keen to introduce 'giant furniture' to improve upon the acoustics, and to make the space less austere, the proportions more human and the space more welcoming. The under-heated concrete floor meant the only way to bring power to the centre of the room (for music and light) was via the ceiling. These challenging practicalities led to a unique solution: Torode's initial idea of three sound-absorbing, egg-shaped structures housing banquettes. 'His brief was the scene from *Pulp Fiction* when Uma Thurman and John Travolta go to Jack Rabbit Slim's diner,' Benchmark's Sean Sutcliffe recalls. 'He wanted to create a diner experience as unusual as that.' The intention was to create a visual magnet inside the space as a substitute for a view. Benchmark developed the brief and it evolved into one grand sculptural gesture. 'We realized that it was feasible to create the illusion of amorphous shapes by using topographical, sliced-up, horizontal or vertical sections – or fins – like map contours,' says Sutcliffe. Benchmark developed the final masterpiece adhering closely to Wells Mackereth's instructions. Wells Mackereth revamped the mezzanine gallery to provide a chic cocktail den offering a moodier ambience and a more laid-back lounge atmosphere than the lighter cafeteria below. 'It's like a minstrel's gallery,' explains Wells, 'it's all about seeing but not being seen; we installed shutters to allow privacy but still create glimpses of the restaurant below.' And it's a pretty spectacular view.

Right:
An aerial view of the central installation shows the constellations of spherical spun-fibreglass and epoxy resin 'Random' light fittings by Moooi, which brighten the room and lower the sight line.

Far right:
The mezzanine level was revamped to create a cocktail bar-cum-minstrel's gallery.

New Baroque

Quilted grey silk, white linen, leather and luminous onyx combine to produce an elegant tableau of 'new baroque' at **Bon**

Bon, Paris, France
March 2000
Philippe Starck

Chic organic restaurant Bon was conceived by über-designer Philippe Starck and restaurateur Laurent Taieb. Having previously commissioned Andreé Putman to create his successful Japanese restaurant Lo Sushi, Taieb clearly understands the power of design. Bon is located in the smart, exclusive 16e arrondissement in the west of Paris and serves a health-conscious organic menu and sushi. As Starck himself says, 'If I leave Bon and can say that I haven't put weight on, then I'll be really happy.' No wonder the glossy posse and fashion pack adore it.

Originally a florist's shop, the 700 square metre (7,500 square foot) restaurant is divided into several separate areas and seats around 200 diners in total. Sumptuous materials reign: quilted grey silk, white linen, leather and luminous onyx combine to produce an elegant tableau of 'new baroque'. This cool, delicate Louis XVI decadence meets *Out of Africa*, with rich, dark timber tables, carved animals and figurines, and in the main dining room a magnificent carved rhino's head presiding above the mantelpiece.

At the front of the restaurant, in keeping with its existing classical features, Starck has introduced bold theatrical flourishes. A high communal banqueting table topped with glowing onyx is lit by silver candelabra; walls are quilted in luxurious grey silk; and a huge, silver-framed mirror maximizes the grandeur of the room. In the centre, an oval 'kaiten' sushi bar presents dishes on a revolving conveyor-belt to diners perched on high stools at the luminous onyx bar. A hallway lined with armoires, and a small boutique selling kitsch Starck products, leads to the rest of the restaurant.

The majority of Bon is accommodated in a lofty, conservatory-style structure to the rear with angled ceilings, staggered levels and an abundance of skylights and windows forming an L-shape around a small courtyard. Preceding the main dining room are two small dining salons on split levels running parallel to the courtyard. A staircase leads up from the entrance hall to a narrow corridor room. Below this, and accessible via a flight of steps, is a second ground-level dining area looking onto the courtyard. Both spaces are shielded from the glare of the sun by diaphanous white window drapes and skylight blinds.

At the rear the level rises again and the space widens to create the largest dining area. Low sofas, plump with fat white pillows, and a roaring hearth convey a casual 'at home' atmosphere. In the centre of the room a cluster of chunky church candles flicker in crystal vases; tea candles on table tops and simple pendant lamps around the periphery of the room provide low, gentle lighting. Shallow alcoves in the timber walls house silver-framed mirrors of tinted glass; leaning at an angle, these offer colourful, dreamlike *Through the Looking Glass* reflections. One deeper alcove accommodates a bright yellow silk-quilted dining booth.

Stairs descend from this room to a spectacular and dazzling double-height salon lined with grey drapes and furnished by a giant 'cross' table. Regal thrones punctuate the four points of the cross, emphasizing its iconic shape. Above the table a silver-framed screen plays abstract images.

The framed picture motif continues in the courtyard outside, but Starck, the master of illusion, is up to his old tricks again: here there are no mirrors or plasma screens, only verdant 'walls' of thyme.

When Morita designs a project the lighting comes first – Anniversaire is no exception

Opposite:
In Room One, three framed
screens play a time-lapse
image of burning candles, on
a continuous loop; the ceiling
frame shows video art.

Right:
The pool of water between
the two dining rooms reflects
the flickering candles, linking
the spaces and enhancing the
sense of romance.

Plan:
The 51-cover restaurant
comprises two separate
rooms, connected by an
entrance corridor decorated
with candlelit pools.

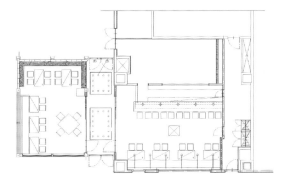

Anniversaire, Tokyo, Japan
October 2001
Glamorous

Japanese designer and founder of Glamorous
Yasumichi Morita is a master of illusion. Since the mid-
1990s his intriguing interiors have enlivened dining scenes
across Asia in Tokyo, Osaka, Kobe and Hong Kong.
Originally a lighting designer, Morita has perfected the art
of deception, using tricks of light and reflection to generate
'phantom depth' and enhance space. When designing a
new project, in Morita's mind the lighting comes first;
Tokyo's Anniversaire is no exception.

This 51-cover Italian restaurant is located on
the first floor of the Omotesando building in Kitaaoyama, a
popular shopping and restaurant district. Glamorous was
commissioned to create a destination restaurant to
complement the existing amenities – a wedding chapel,
a bridal boutique, a party hall and a café. In response to
the owner's wish 'that people … visit the restaurant to
celebrate their anniversary or special occasions', Morita
has used baroque silver elements and candles throughout
the scheme to evoke a sense of romance and celebration.

Grand silver pillars constructed from timber
stacking frames form the main entrance, which leads into
a limestone-paved corridor. Anniversaire is divided between
a formal dining room (Room Two) with a terrace on the left
and a funkier, more casual dining room (Room One) on
the right; they are intrinsically linked by the candle motif.
A bed of candles arranged in square pools between the
two areas adds illumination and spatial depth. Floor-to-
ceiling windows afford a clear view of each room and the
flickering pools of light between them.

Inside both rooms the magnified (time-lapse)
image of five burning candles projected onto screens
provides a dramatic visual focus and brings the interiors
to life. By combining modern technology with the most
ancient form of light, the naked flame, Morita creates a
magical effect. Room One houses three angled screens set
high above diners' heads, and a large central ceiling frame
displays video art. The double-length screen in Room Two
is a mirror image, but in duplicate. Each visual appears like
a classical painting, hanging within a heavy silver frame
echoing the grand entrance pillars, the waiter service
stations and the candelabra.

These grand and classical illuminations contrast
brilliantly with the simplicity of each room. Custom-made,
Burmese padouk-timber-topped tables are teamed with
fine dining chairs in Room Two and with white Bertoia side-
chairs in the more playful Room One. In keeping with the
retro feel of this room, Morita has custom made the lights
in table lamp and arching 'Arco' pendant form. Fabricated
by sandwiching pasta between two acrylic cylinders, these
exude a warm, 1960s orange glow. Yet again, Glamorous
lighting is the main attraction. Bon Anniversaire.

Supperclub Roma occupies an ancient building full of character that belies its 21st-century interior

Left:
La Salle Neige is, unsurprisingly, all white, with an Italian white marble floor and two giant bunk beds lining each side; 'elephant drum' tables double as dancing podiums late in the evening.

Supperclub Roma, Rome, Italy
June 2002
Concrete Architectural Associates

Architects of cool Dutch firm Concrete pioneered the trend for extreme louche dining. Since opening in 1999, their original Supperclub in Amsterdam has spawned imitators across the world, proof that in this technospeedy, frenetic world we all love the chance to take things lying down occasionally. Bedding diners proved so successful that Supperclub owner Bert van der Leden commissioned Concrete to create a sequel. For their repeat performance Concrete brought the Roman-inspired dining concept back home to Rome.

The beauty of both Supperclubs lies in their surroundings. Like its Dutch sibling, Supperclub Roma occupies the basement of an ancient building full of character that belies its 21st-century interior. Dating back to the 15th century and located in the old city, the host building is rumoured to have been built on the site of the bath-house of Emperor Nero. More recently the space operated as a hardware store, with many of the original features concealed. Concrete's renovation involved restoring the early architecture, bringing the entrance

back to its original position and installing completely new services, such as the kitchen and toilets. 'It was hell; the walls are 1.5 metres (5 feet) thick and it took us 16 months, whereas Amsterdam took ten days,' explains Rob Wagemans, co-founder of Concrete with Gilian Schofer.

Despite this, Wagemans feels that the Italian model is a great improvement, offering diners a higher level of escapism: 'The route you have to follow before you go to dinner is much more dramatic; we used the architecture much better than we did in Amsterdam'. The simple, classical entrance lobby entitled Heaven's Door (Porte du Ciel) is intriguing: the 15th-century house was constructed cloister-style, and this was originally the street entrance to the courtyard, where the horses would be tethered. On arrival guests pass through Heaven's Door first: 'There is always art, a performance or something happening, so you get confused and disorientated, leave everything behind and start your new experience here.'

Supperclub Roma is modelled on its predecessor, so there is a replica 'Bar Rouge' complete with all-red interior, glowing neon 'Bar' sign, glitterball and go-go dancing pole. Diners enter this crimson decadence next, the curtains are closed and cocktails are served. At suppertime everyone is invited to bed in La Salle Neige, a bleached white space with giant steel bunk-beds lining each side. Twin translucent stepladders fixed to each framework provide access to the upper levels.

It's a soothing experience. Shoes are removed and people recline against large pillows; changing LED lighting drenches the interior in different pastel shades, and ambient lounge music sets a mellow vibe. The ultimate in stress-free dining, the menu is pre-set and everyone eats the same 5-course meal, enhancing the community spirit. There are several conventional 'elephant drum' dining tables in the centre, custom-made and robust enough to become dancing podiums when the venue transforms into a club later on. Pure white Verner Panton chairs complete the dreamy *mise en scène*.

Le Bed Baroque is the new feature unique to Supperclub Roma. One colossal super-bed fills a neighbouring room; surrounded by a halo of light (recessed beneath the metal frame), it appears to float. 'We always try to push the boundaries and with this extra space we thought, let's turn the Supperclub inside out. Instead of the beds on the side, we'll have one big bed in the middle,' recalls Wagemans. Initial responses to the idea were less than enthusiastic, but as Wagemans says, 'Now by the end of the night most people would love to sit in the big bed; it creates a special chemistry between people. It's great.' In the future Concrete plans to take the Supperclub experience outside, taking alfresco decadence to its limits.

Left:
Heaven's Door at Supperclub Roma, which occupies a building that dates back to the 15th century.

Opposite:
Le Bed Baroque can accommodate 45 people for dining, dancing or just reclining to admire the ceiling masterpiece and multicoloured lighting.

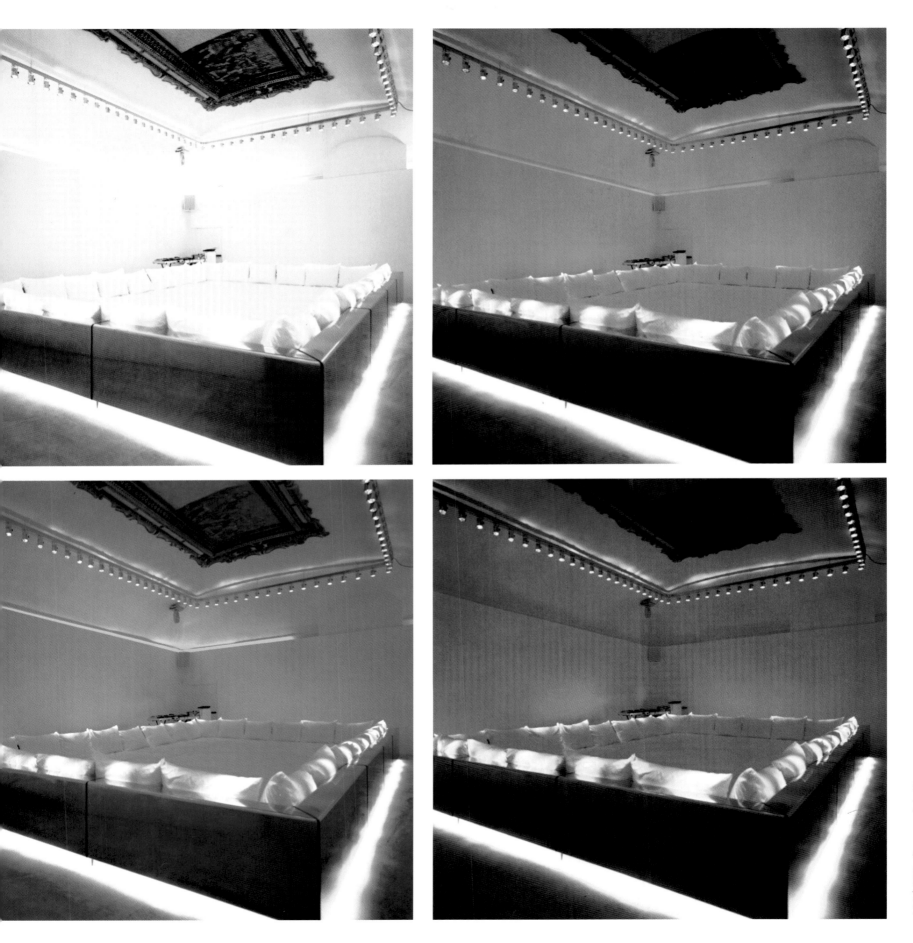

Sketch offers an escapist parade of experiences, from twisted tearooms to outer-space bars, decadent dining rooms and bejewelled toilets

Left:
The Gallery restaurant functions as a video gallery by day, housing 12 projectors capable of creating a continuous 2.7 metre (9 foot) high image on a white Barrisol material that wraps around the room.

Right:
Ron Arad's reception desk in the entrance hall, reflected in Vincent Leroy's 'kinetic sculpture'; the work is kept in perpetual motion and faced with double mirrors, so that its image echoes into infinity.

Sketch, London, UK
January 2003
Mourad Mazouz (Noé Duchafour-Lawrence, Gabhan O'Keefe & Jurgen Bey)

Sketch is an eclectic temple, devoted to avant-garde food, music, art and design. Its name describes the transitory nature of this five-part emporium: conceived as a 'work in progress', it 'will constantly evolve like a painting that never dries'. French-Algerian restaurateur Mourad Mazouz recalls the project's early days: 'Sketch came together really organically … we bought the Grade II listed building and submitted drawings to English Heritage, but they objected to lots of our ideas, so we did a lot of sketches.' The process of renovating the 1,860 square metre (20,000 square foot) Georgian property, built in 1779 by architect James Wyatt, became a monumental task. Momo intended to spend £5 million ($7.5 million) on the scheme, but the refurbishment process was significantly delayed by the necessity of extensive restructuring and costs soared: Sketch finally emerged four years and £10 million ($15 million) later.

The core concept was simple. 'My idea of London was like this building, a place with very deep tradition,' says Momo, 'but when I arrived in London during the late 1990s there was also all this design, art and music that was very, very modern. So the idea was to combine

tradition and modernity.' To achieve this he commissioned a cast of designers, sculptors and artists, most notably Parisian sculptor/designer Noé Duchafour-Lawrence, responsible for most of the ground floor except the Parlour pâtisserie and tearoom (by Jurgen Bey of Amsterdam's Droog design), and Irish designer Gabhan O'Keefe, who created the first-floor Lecture Room and Library restaurant. Michelin three-star Parisian chef Pierre Gagnaire has created the entire food concept for Sketch.

In the wide Georgian corridor a series of arched niches houses sculptures by Jurgen Bey; a door on the right leads into the Parlour overlooking the street. This pâtisserie and tearoom presents delicate savouries and cakes in glass display counters like precious jewels. Here Bey captures the classic-modern aesthetic by revitalizing ('re-skinning') ornate domestic chairs, tables, brocade lamps and crystal chandeliers with modern materials. Portraits lifted from paintings by Dutch masters adorn the upholstered chair backs, lending the room a quirky, inhabited character even when empty. Original wall mouldings maintain an air of old-fashioned Georgian gentility – juxtaposed with objects exuding a radical 21st-century edge.

En route to the other areas patrons pass a reception desk by Ron Arad and a 'kinetic sculpture' by Vincent Leroy set into the wall. The cloakroom attendants are framed by a 'floating' futuristic white counter-cum-sculpture. A set of doors leads through to the West Bar, Gallery and East Bar: originally a yard and stables, these spaces now feature glazed dome ceilings and majestic barrel skylights.

The Gallery restaurant designed by Momo and Duchafour-Lawrence operates as a video art gallery during the day. After 5 p.m. the Gallery morphs into a restaurant and white furniture is arranged to accommodate 150 diners. A modular high communal table snakes through the room, with further tables and Louis XVI-style chairs of varying heights adding depth; elsewhere, seating is provided by low banquettes and chairs. After 11 p.m. the Gallery transforms again, this time into a lounge bar. The furniture is rearranged, the banquettes become beds and a DJ plays electronic-electro and house.

Above left:
In the Parlour, wall niches, table tops and display cases are decorated with a heritage-grey plastic that bears a pretty flock-patterned design; an 18th-century motif of a couple taking tea is reversed and repeated.

Far left:
The futuristic cloakroom counter is fixed to the ceiling and floor by a central rod, thus allowing it to rotate 360 degrees.

Right:
The Lecture Room exudes luxury, with horizontal gold bands lining the walls, mirror panelling, exquisite lanterns and ruby velvet armchairs.

Left:
In the bejewelled toilets, opulent webs of crystals and sparkling floral patterns can be found; even the toilet paper is suspended from the ceiling on crystal bead chains.

Right:
A toilet pod on a mezzanine level looms large, reflected in a convex vanity mirror.

On either side of the Gallery are the 45-capacity West Bar and 35-capacity East Bar. The West Bar is bathed in a gradient of colour, fading from deep red at ceiling level to white at the floor, which curves up to form the long bar counter. Reupholstered vintage 1960s and 1970s furniture and lighting sourced by Momo at Parisian flea markets lend a funky, retro-futuro feel here.

The East Bar, by contrast, is pure sci-fi: a surreal white igloo structure with a sunken bar and a colourful fresco on the domed ceiling. Twin flights of stairs curve up on either side to pod toilets (which resemble giant eggs) on a mezzanine level. This *Space Odyssey* invention was a solution to a very practical problem, 'I didn't want yet another room with a large capacity and so needed to reduce the size,' explains Mazouz; 'I also like the idea of creating toilets with a communal area.'

On another mezzanine floor, accessible from the entrance hall, are the true lavatorial gems. Here, young jewellery designer Mehbs Yaqub has created glittering jewel-boxes clad in backlit coloured glass encrusted with over £35,000 ($54,000) of Swarovski crystals. All befitting the flamboyant luxury of the 70-cover Lecture Room and Library upstairs.

Left:
In the East Bar, the bartender serves drinks from a sunken bar-pit.

Bottom:
A thin red line of shelving stands out against the bleeding red-fading-to-white walls of the West Bar.

Right:
The East Bar's igloo entrance: inside, on the mezzanine, are ovoid toilet cubicles, which look like giant eggs – the six blue ones are for the gentlemen, while the other six, for the ladies, are bathed in pink light.

Gabhan O'Keefe's plush, jewel-hued interiors were inspired by Gagnaire's 'food as art' creations, priced at over £100 ($150) per head. A coffered dome imbues the Lecture Room with a formal grandeur, enriched by taffeta lanterns, ruby velvet chairs and an elaborate, hand-painted 'reflection' on the carpet below. The mirror tiles covering the back wall maximize space and glamour.

At the rear is the smaller Library dining room lined with white leather padding studded with tiny convex mirrors. The fireplaces are flanked by towering vases framed dramatically within brightly patterned wall niches. Large Art Deco-style convex mirrors give fish-eye reflections of the room. Lavish textures continue in the neighbouring smoking room, where patrons can recline on O'Keefe's asymmetrical sofas and chairs.

Mazouz and his team have created an escapist parade of experiences, from twisted tearooms to outer-space bars, decadent dining rooms and bejewelled toilets – an eclectic backdrop that encourages guests to play and perform. But don't be surprised if by the time you visit Sketch has undergone another metamorphosis and been sketched anew.

The most eye-catching elements of Gong are the ceiling 'raft lights' fringed with chrome beading

Gong, Glasgow, UK
October 2001
United Designers Ltd

The long-standing partnership between Glasgow's G1 Group and the London-based design consultancy United Designers has produced a veritable empire of hip dining and drinking venues in the cosmopolitan Scottish city. These include the new baroque Polo Lounge, the Moroccan Den Babaza, the grand classical Corinthian and the Spanish haçienda-style Arta. Having been credited by the city council for regenerating the Merchants City area of Glasgow, G1 has now looked further afield for disused buildings ripe for renovation. One such site was an old cinema, originally built in 1918 and situated in the city's lively, student-orientated West End.

United Designers converted the space into a dramatic 540 square metre (5,800 square foot) restaurant seating 110 diners, with 'bookend' mezzanine bars at either end seating a further 68 patrons. The major structural work involved levelling the sloping auditorium floor and installing a new timber one, allowing for varying levels to create drama. The silver screen is replaced by the altar-like Stage Bar at one end, accessible via a small flight of steps and enclosed by low, etched glass screens. Huge, opulent swathes of red velvet theatrically frame the marble bar itself. A 'mobile screen' backdrop of suspended strands of bronze and orange acrylic panels enlivens this classic bar.

Diners are accommodated on banquettes and chairs arranged in 'caged' compartments in the midst of the space, with service routes delineated in limestone circulating around them. The upper halves of the dark timber partitions are punctuated with slender metal rods, sprayed bronze, shooting in random directions to form crazy screens between the compartments. Recessed lighting floods up through holes punched in the bases of the screens, illuminating this unusual detail and affording a sense of intimacy without obstructing views of the restaurant and bar mezzanines. A larger lounge bar at the rear is furnished with custom-made leather club chairs and slim, marble-topped cocktail tables.

The walls are decorated with mirrored panelling and huge pipes inspired by Tibetan prayer scrolls. But by far the most eye-catching elements of Gong are the ceiling 'raft lights' fringed with chrome beading. Programmed to gradually change colour over the course of the evening, these send out diffuse hues of orange, purple and blue, allowing the atmosphere to be fully controlled in the absence of natural light.

Left:
Transformed from an old cinema, the dining area is flanked by two raised bar areas; an 'altar bar' at one end and a higher, mezzanine-level lounge bar at the other.

Right:
The dramatic Stage Bar replaces the silver screen and features a backdrop of acrylic panels that reflect the light and create a sense of movement.

Les Trois Garçons brims with decadence... a glittering gem in London's East End

**Les Trois Garçons & Loungelover,
London, UK**
October 2000, March 2003
Hassan Abdullah, Stefan Karlson
& Michel Lasserre

Part of the charm of Les Trois Garçons lies in the sheer incongruity of its location: like a diamond in the dust it is a glittering gem set in the grimy backstreets of London's East End. It virtually stands alone in the wasteland between the vibrant bars and curry houses of Brick Lane and trendy Shoreditch. Not that this has stopped the bijou French restaurant becoming the favourite haunt of fashionistas, designers and London's beau monde. However, judging by the diversity of its patrons, the eccentric theatricality of the space appeals to the artist and performer in us all – and this was the idea. As they say, 'The intention is to break away from the more formal and austere minimal effect created by the current *enfants* of the restaurant world, and bring some character and a sense of playfulness into mealtimes.'

Les Trois Garçons was created by a trio of antique dealers: Swede Stefan Karlson, Frenchman Michel Lasserre and Malay Hassan Abdullah. Before setting up their antique-dealing business Karlson worked in tourism, Lasserre managed a restaurant in Paris and Abdullah worked as an interior designer producing classic hotel interiors. The corner site, purchased as a domestic

residence and business, had an interesting history: 'It's a listed Victorian pub,' explains Abdullah, 'but before that it was a Huguenot tavern that was demolished in 1880; hey used part of the bricks to build the pub. It's probably the last remaining pub in [the borough of] Tower Hamlets of this age.'

Due to the historic nature of the property, the first task was restoration. 'We had to reinstate the bar back to its original position, replace two of the gilded Victorian glass brewery mirrors that had been stolen, strip back the wood and ceilings and repair the floor,' says Abdullah, reckoning that this process cost approximately £300,000 ($460,000). Next came the concept, a deliberate departure from restrained modern interiors. Abdullah explains this 'new baroque': 'English pubs are beautiful but quite grim and heavy; I wanted to glamorize it, that's why I added crystals and stuffed animals dressed in tiaras, to make it a bit more fun. Why take everything so seriously? I want a bit of wit: when you go out to eat it's about escaping, it's about fantasy.'

Les Trois Garçons is brimming with decadence. The large pub windows are dressed with strands of crystal beads 'to camouflage the greyness of outside'. Among the taxidermy and tiaras menagerie are a bulldog with fairy wings, a gibbon in glittering jewels, Quentin the crocodile balanced on a grand piano and the resident tiger prowling in a diamanté necklace. Lighting is extravagant: cascades of crystal beads drip down from square lighting panels, and Murano glass chandeliers redolent of white feathers produce a gentle glow. In the centre of the space a collection of delicate beaded handbags dangles like a twinkling art installation.

Left:
A giant Chanel clock is the centrepiece of the bar.

Above:
Heartstopper mirrors side by side in the sexy toilets of Les Trois Garçons.

Right:
If bulldogs could fly: this bejewelled mutt stands guard at the entrance, against elaborately gilded Victorian glass brewery mirrors.

Abdullah says of collecting: 'I keep adding things and am running out of room … I just can't resist buying beautiful things.' This has led to the addition of Loungelover, a maximalist restaurant and lounge bar tucked down the cobbled side street behind Les Trois Garçons. This former meat-processing warehouse exudes the same bountiful philosophy. Equally eclectic, the sumptuous 250-capacity space is overflowing with exquisite antiques and bizarre objets trouvés from Italy, Sweden and France – a sparkling confirmation that the three creators are the masters of maximalism.

It's very Moulin Rouge but with a decidedly savvy Brit edge. Ornaments include a child's medical model toy, no doubt a knowing wink to Damien Hirst's *Hymn*. Some items have been customized, 'We've given things a twist,' says Abdullah, 'such as the 18th-century Swedish furniture I've upholstered in fresh, modern leather It's more durable than chintz or damask, and it's fun to have bright leathers on such old pieces.' Other adapted items include an eighteenth-century mirror, 'I found it boring, so commissioned some guys to mosaic the glass.' It has pride of place in the VIP 'cage', a side room protected by prison-like bars that fold back into side shutters, which are incorporated into an antique façade salvaged from a French butcher's shop. Lit by a bevy of crystal chandeliers, candelabra, Murano lights and Oriental lanterns, Loungelover offers extravagant escapism rivalled only by Les Trois Garçons.

Below left:
Decadence on display, all carefully arranged to encourage 'lounge-loving'.

Below right:
The VIP cage room is protected by prison-like bars that slide back.

Opposite:
Loungelover restaurant and lounge bar sparkles with lighting, from the custom-designed crystal chandeliers to the constellation of mini-crowns, created by Abdullah, and the movie-set spotlights; 'Going out is like being on stage. You go to see and be seen.'

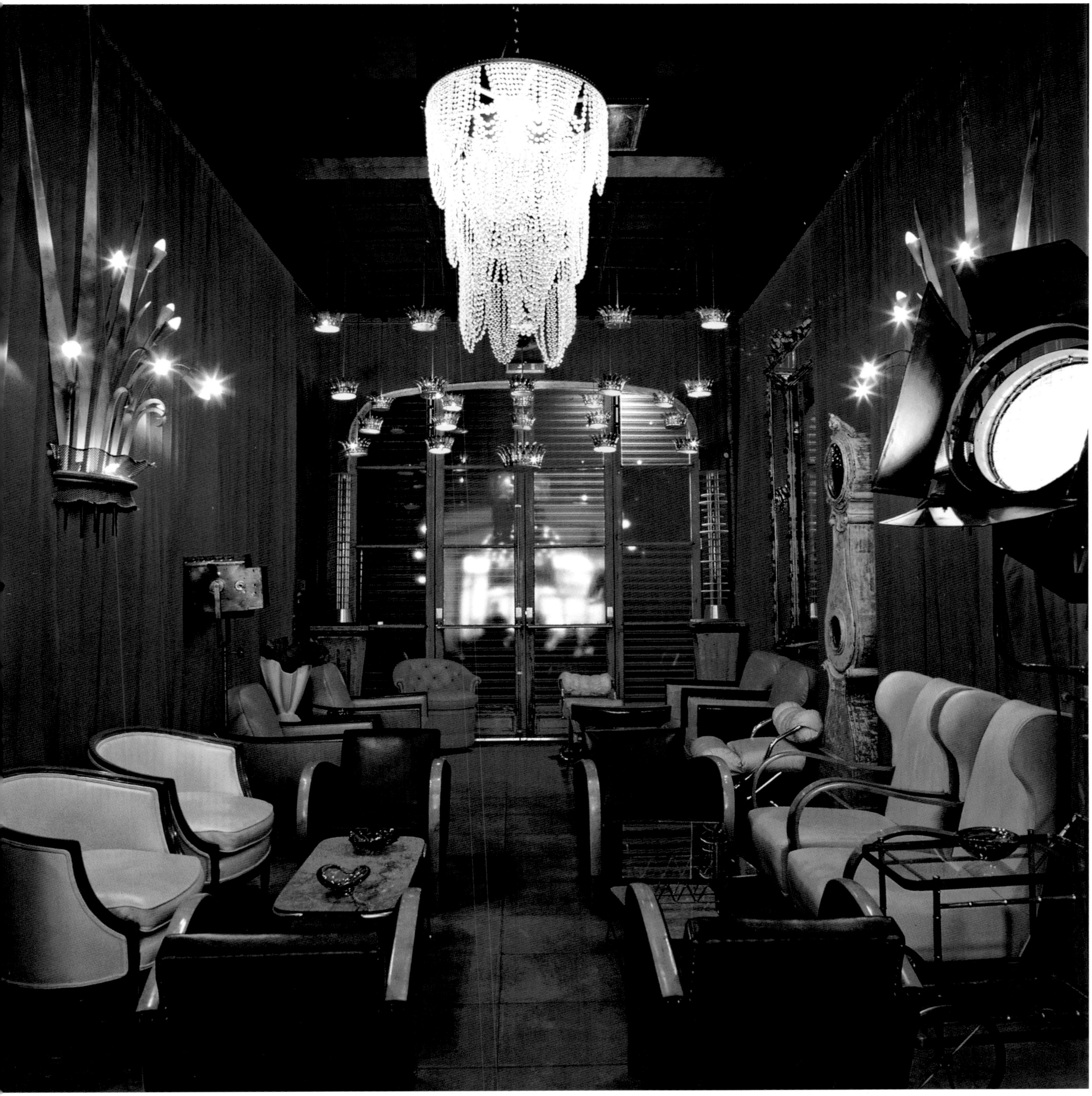

At Plaza Athénée Jouin had to take care to integrate modern details without altering the classic setting

Left:
Colossal chandeliers are veiled in metallic organza, a modern skin that tempers a classic design.

Right:
Jouin's mantelpiece masterpiece: an abstract orange clock in detail.

Plaza Athénée, Paris, France
September 2000
Patrick Jouin

If hotels, restaurants and bars have become today's entertainment, then the headline double act is surely hip hotelier Ian Schrager and design maverick Philippe Starck. Perhaps it's logical then that one of Schrager's partners, multi-starred Michelin chef Alain Ducasse (of Spoon at The Sanderson Hotel, London), and an ex-member of Starck's studio, design polymath Patrick Jouin, should also have formed a similarly successful double act.

Originally built in 1911, the Plaza Athénée long enjoyed its position as Paris's premier luxury hotel, catering to the rich and famous who adored the smart Avenue Montaigne address and its proximity to exclusive couture boutiques. However, the hotel market underwent a considerable renaissance during the 1990s and as a result Plaza Athénée's appeal began to fade. The management initiated an extensive revamp in 1999 and Alain Ducasse was invited to modernize the existing restaurant.

Ducasse chose Jouin to assist him – they had already completed a contemporary renovation of the traditional interior at Restaurant 59 Poincaré. At Plaza Athénée Jouin had to achieve an equally sensitive transformation, integrating modern details within the classic setting. Instead of embellishing the gilded mouldings and ornate cornices with yet more fanciful decoration, Jouin has essentially muted the interior and reined in the extravagance by adding neutral materials and wrapping elements in a modern skin.

Four grey felt folding screens define the spaces between the dining room and kitchens, while also acting as sound absorbers. Elegant silk-upholstered Louis XV dining chairs have been clad in a pewter finish, providing a cool, understated look in contrast to the baroque excesses of the palatial dining room. The centre of the carpet is emblazoned with a large orange cross. 'Ducasse told me never to put a table in the centre of the room, because people don't feel comfortable,' explains Jouin. 'Usually people fill the space with flowers, but I wanted the emptiness so I put the cross there instead.'

The original colossal chandeliers remain, but sheathed in cylindrical metallic organza veils to appear like 21st-century holograms of their former selves. Jouin added lighting of a more human scale in the form of Starck's office desk lamps around the periphery of the room, as 'homage to my master' (*Frame*, no. 29, November/December 2002). The old, gilt-framed oil paintings on the walls were replaced by stark, unframed contemporary photographic portraits by Thomas Duval.

On the marble mantelpiece is a handless clock that 'ambiguously tells the time': 'When people visit an exclusive gastronomic restaurant time has to be disregarded; you will not count every second that you are there, but every second you spend there has to be ncredible, time disappears,' says Jouin. 'Everything else is very baroque and you have this pure object that is an enigma for people; they know it's in the place of a clock and so maybe they understand it is a clock but they are not sure.' This abstract timepiece also symbolizes the timeless quality of Jouin's old-meets-new interior.

In May 2001 Jouin was asked to apply a similar treatment to the Bar du Plaza. Here he created two distinct spaces within the listed wood-panelled interior. The lively bar area features a luminous bar fashioned from glass by Patrick Desserme to resemble a giant block of ice. Running parallel to this is a high drinking table accompanied by pewter stools and lit by small, delicate chandeliers in Murano glass.

In the warmer, more subdued lounge Jouin has teamed club armchairs by Cassina. Seventeenth-century landscapes by Claude Gellée (Le Lorrain) have been transformed by graphic designer Philippe David into scenic backdrops and framed in grey velvet. Sofas are set deep into the velvet frames, transporting patrons into landscapes of the past.

Juxtaposed with these historical images is the futuristic giant 'bathtub' lamp. 'People feel more comfortable close to walls; they don't like to stand in the middle of the room, so as a solution I created a space within the space,' says Jouin. Fabricated from white fibreglass, the lamp sends out a diffuse ambient light that drenches the lounge with mutating hues, from cool blues to sunset orange. 'I wanted to introduce an enigma like the clock into this classic interior, an object that is the total opposite of everything and so big you can't miss it, so you are in the present, but also somewhere between the future and the past. You don't know where you are, you could be in a dream.'

Below:
A fibreglass sculpture-cum-light installation like an upturned bath casts a changing light onto the lounge.

Picture Credits

Archipress (129); Archiv Archipress/artur (126–128 bottom); Mark Ballogg (17); James Balston (12); Courtesy Balthazar (15 left); Courtesy Berk Communications (32–35); Bettmann/Corbis (11); Luc Boegly/Archipress (74–75, 84–85); N. Borel (128 top); Bridgeman Art Library – British Museum, London (8); Bridgeman Art Library – Guildhall Library, Corporation of London (10); Bridgeman Art Library – Museo Archeologico Nazionale, Naples (6); Bridgeman Art Library – private collection (9); Oscar Brito (94–97); Friedrich Busam (86–87, 90–91, 110–111); Mike Butler (78–81); Joseph Chartouni (132–135); Courtesy Concrete Architectural Associates (36–37, 164–167); Richard Davies (175); Michel Denancé (158–161); Todd Eberle (16 top right); Andrea Flak (112–113); Klaus Frahm/artur (140–143); Michael Franke (39 left, 40, 42–43); David Frutos Ruiz (92–93); Jeff Goldberg/ESTO (16 left); Marcus Gortz (82–83); Alan Hindle/David Yeo (52–55); Eduard Hueber (116–119); Werner Huthmacher (108–109); David M. Joseph (20–23, 68–69, 150–153); Nicholas Kane/ARCAID (15 right); Simon Kenny (120–121); Joe Kesrwani (122–125); Scott Kester (76–77); Eric Laignel (24–25, 184–187); Eric Laignel/Evon Dion (144–149); Andrew Lamb (14 left); Commissioned photography – Rob Lawson (3, 5, 18, 66, 116, 160); Rob Lawson (182–183); Jorg Lehman (58–61); Olivier Martin-Gambier/Archipress (44–48); Michael Moran (14 middle); Nacasa and Partners, Inc. (26–31, 162–163); Peter Paige (56–57); Matteo Piazza (102–107); Yael Pincus (180); Eugeni Pons (50–51, 100–101); Saint Blanquat (49); Liberty Silver (154–155); Doug Snower (130–131); Courtesy Philippe Starck (16 bottom right); Martyn Rose (168–174); Thomas Stewart (98–99); Hisao Suzuki (136–139); Eric Thorburn © The Glasgow Picture Library (176–177); Courtesy Le Train Bleu (13 bottom); Simon Upton (13 top); Paul Warchol (70–73); Rodney Weidland and Rodney Evans (62–65); World of Interiors – Tom Mannion (178–179, 181).

Restaurant Index

Furniture Suppliers: Coexistence
Spun-fibreglass Lighting Suppliers: Moooi

Centrale, Beirut
Bernard Khoury Architect
Project team: Bernard Khoury (Project Architect), Fadi Sarieddine (Project Manager), Patrick Mezher, Michele Maria, Balsam Ariss, Yasmina Khalifesh
Client: Centrale
Main Contractor: ENG Elie Abdelnoor
Consultants: A.C.I.D.
Graphic Design: Black Trombone
Furniture: Interdesign

Coconut Groove, Frankfurt
www.bender-design.de
www.coconut-groove.de
Bender Design
Client: Jüb GmbH
Outside Chairs: 'Tom Vac', Ron Arad for Vitra

Comerç 24, Barcelona
Architects: Xavier Abellàn, Anna Rius
Interior Designer: Alfons Tost
Project Team: Lali Canosa, (Lighting Designer), Dr. Marcel Li Rius (Industrial Engineer)
Client: Carles Abellàn, Toro Taller de Cuina S.L.
Construction: Juan Rodriguez, Construcciones Macor

Craft, New York
www.bentelandbentel.com
www.craftrestaurant.com
Architect/Interior Designer/Lighting Designer: Bentel & Bentel Architects/Planners AIA LLP
Project Team: Peter Bentel, Paul Bentel, Carol Rusche (Collaborating Principals), Susan Nagle (Interior Designer), Thomas O'Connor, Boone Lo, Christopher Hinchey
Client: Foodcraft LLC
General Contractor: Jadum Construction Co.
Engineers: Altieri, Sebor, Wieber LLC (M/E/P/S), Koutsoubis, Alonso Associates (Structural), Food Service Concepts (Food Service), TR Technologies (Audio)
Leather Wall, Banquettes, Wine Wall and Bar, Bronze Sinks, Imbuia Cabinetry, Cherry Dining Tables: Bentel & Bentel
Chairs: Arper
Barstools: Danko
Stone Floors in Bathroom: Lava Salte from Stone Source
Bronze Egress Doors: Total Door Systems

Dos Caminos, New York
www.brguestrestaurants.com
Yabu Pushelberg
Project design team: George Yabu, Glenn Pushelberg, Fabienne Moureaux, Andrew Kimber, Grace Plawinski, Gary Chan
Technical team: Robert Auger, Shane Park, Karl Travis, Eric Lam, Catherine Chan
Project management: Kevin Storey, Christina Gustavs
Client: Stephen Hanson, B.R. Guest, Inc.

El Japonès, Barcelona
www.grupotragaluz.com
Sandra Tarruella and Isabel López
Collaborator: Emma Massana
Client: Grupo Tragaluz
Main Contractor: Closa
Engineer: GDR Instalaciones
Graphic Designer: Mario Eskenazi

Fritz Fischer, Berlin
www.fritz-fischer.de
Bürozentral
Project Team: Karin Sander, Thomas Wolter, Uli Lechtleitner
Site Architects: Aukett & Heese GmbH
Project Team: Stefan Pehle, Victoria zu Castell, Phillip Knopp
Client: Universal Entertainment, GmbH
Main Contractor: Connex GmbH

Project Credits

Anniversaire, Tokyo
www.glamorous.co.jp
Glamorous Co. Ltd.
Project Team: Yasumichi Morita, Kazuhiro Shimada
Client: Aoki International Co. Ltd.
Main Contractor: Mitsui Designtec Co. Ltd.
Lighting design: Daiko Electric Co. Ltd.

Bed Supperclub, Bangkok
www.bedsupperclub.com
www.orbitdesignstudio.com
Orbit Design Studio (Architecture, Interiors and Graphic Identity)
Project Team: Christopher Redpath, Simon Drogemuller (interiors)
Project Management: Orbit Design Studio
Structural Engineer: Warnes Associates
M&E: EFS
Kitchen: Sommerville

Blue Fin, New York
www.brguestrestaurants.com
Architect: Brennan Beer Gorman Architects
Project Team: Mario LaGuardia, Kevin Brown
Interior Design: Yabu Pushelberg
Project Team: George Yabu, Glenn Pushelberg, Marcia MacDonald, Mary Mark, Reg Andrade, Sunny Leung, Marc Gaudet, Eduardo Figueredo, Kevin Storey
Client: Stephan Hanson, B. R. Guest, Inc.
Main Contractors: J. T. Magen & Company, Pancor Industries Ltd., Martin Thomas Contracting, Inc.
Kitchen Consultant: Romano Gatland
Structural Engineer: Desimone Consulting Engineers
Mechanical and Electrical Engineers: Lehr Associates, Consulting Engineers David Scher, Subvoyant
Special Finishes: Moss & Lam, Inc.
Pendant Light Sculptures/Fixture: Unit 5 Metal Fabricators
Special Light Fixtures: TPL Marketing, Inc.
School of Fish Sculpture: Hirotoshi Sawada, Studio Sawada Design

Bon, Paris
www.philippe-starck.com
www.bon.fr

Café Etienne Marcel, Paris
www.mmparis.com
Pierre Huyghe, Philippe Parreno & M/M (Mathias Augustyniak & Michael Amzalag)
Client: Thierry Costes

Cafeteria, London
www.cafeteria.co.uk
Wells Mackereth Architects
Client: Bob's Restaurants Ltd.
Contractor: Power Building Services
Structural Engineer: Haskins Robinson Waters
Specialist Bar Supplier: Airedale Catering Ltd.
Specialist Furniture Design and Construction: Benchmark

Technical Engineering: Büro Happold
Project Control: Jones Lang Laselle
Carpenter: Ideal Innenausbau (furniture)
Fibreglass Wall: Ausstellungsmanufaktur Hertzer

Fusion, Hamburg
www.matteothun.com
www.side-hamburg.de
Matteo Thun Partners
Collaborators: Jan Störmer
Project Team: Archim Schneider, Thomas Mau, Matthias Latzke, Christine Hilgenstock
Seaside Project Team: Herr Neitzel, Frau Gröger, Herr Beyer, Herr Fraune, Frau Rink
Side Hotel Project Team: H. Starke, F. Müller
Client: Seaside Hotels
Construction of Common Spaces: Göbel Jirka, Fladnitz a.d.t.
Lighting: Zumtobel/Staff, Luxmate
Air Conditioning: Zent-Frenger, Neue Wilmstorf
Media: Dekom
Natural Stone: Azienda Dankert
Construction: Overmann

Georges, Paris
Jakob + MacFarlane
Client: Thierry Costes

Ginto, Tokyo
www.glamorous.co.jp
Glamorous Co. Ltd
Project Team: Yasumichi Morita, Takuma Sato
Client: Ramla Co. Ltd.
Main Contractor: Ideal Co.
Lighting Design: Kenji Ito (Maxray Inc.)
Contributing Artist: Yumi Tohyama

Gong, Glasgow
www.united-designers.com
United Designers Europe Ltd.
Client: G1 Group
Contractor: McMillan Contracts

Hakkasan, London
Executive Architects: Jestico & Whiles
Designer: Christian Liaigre
Client: Alan Yau
Main Contractor: Pat Carter Shopfitting Ltd.
M&E Engineers: The Building Services Group
Quantity Surveyors: Keogh Edwards

Herzblut, Hamburg
www.herzblut-st-pauli.de
www.mozer.com
Jordan Mozer & Associates
Collaborator: Christoph Strenger
Client: Gastro Consulting HH
Investor: Astra Brauerei
Project Management: Gastro Consulting HH

Icebergs, Sydney
www.idrb.com
Lazzarini Pickering Architetti
Project Team: Carl Pickering, Carlo Lazzarini, Barbara Fragale, Giuseppe Postet
Executive Architect: Tanner Architects
Project Team: Xandra Lim (Project Architect), Tony Kemeny, Michael Clarke, Ian Leung
Client: Maurice Terzini
Lighting Design: Lazzarini Pickering Architetti
Lighting Consultant: Clipsal
Services Consultants: Scott Wilson, Irwin Johnston
Builder: Easton Builders NSW
Project Manager: MsW Projects
Structural Engineer: Van der Meer Bonser
Acoustic Consultant: PKA Acoustic Consulting
Fabric Research and Coordination: Skye McCardle

Jones, Philadelphia
www.scheferdesign.com
www.podrestaurant.citysearch.com
David Schefer Design
Project Team: David and Eve-Lynn Schefer
Client: Stephen Starr, Starr Restaurant Organization
Main Contractor: Michael Palermo for SRO, Sansei Builders
Lighting Designer: Focus Lighting
Banquette Fabrication: Dine-Rite
Banquette Fabric: Maharam
Chairs: Format
Table Top/Bar Top: Table Topics
Bar Stools: Mr Barstool
Carpet: Lane's
Mural Fabrication: Vomela
Mural Image: Corbis
Cork Flooring: Expanko
Stone of Columns and Wall: Cultured Stone
Light Fixtures: Custom Design by Schefer Design
Lighting Fabrication: Owen Kamihima
Night Lights: Illuminart

Les Cols, Olot City
RCR Aranda Pigem Vilalta Architects
Project Team: Rafael Aranda, Carmen Pigem, Ramon Vilalta
Client: Fina Puigdevall and Manel Puigvert
Main Contractor: Miquel Subiràs
Structure: Blázquez-Guanter
Ironwork: Metàl Liques Olot
Toilets: Lagares SA
Washbasins and Urinals: RCR Architects
Visualization: J. Padrosa

Les Trois Garçons and Loungelover, London
www.lestroisgarcons.com
Owned and designed by: Hassan Abdullah, Stefan Karlson & Michel Lasserre

Locanda Locatelli, London
www.davidcollins.com
www.locandalocatelli.com
Interior Design, Project Management and Lighting Design: David Collins Architecture and Design
Client: Churchill Inter-Continental Hotel
Furniture: David Collins
Main Contractor: PBH Shopfitters Ltd.

Lupino, Barcelona
Studiox Design Group
Project Team: Ellen Rapelius, Xavier Franquesa
Client: Lupino S.L.
Collaborator: Miquel Casaponsa
Main Contractor: CETA
Artist: Louise Sudell
Technical Consultant: BIM Estudis Tècnics
Acoustic Consultant: Querol Consultors, S.L.
Chairs: Model 03 design: Marten van Severen, manufacture: Vitra
Lighting: Gaudir Il.luminacio S.L.
Pavement: Pavindus

Monastrell, Alicante
Javier Garcia-Solera Vera Arquitecto
Client: Benimagrell 52 S.L.
Collaborator: Deborah Domingo (Architect)

Morimoto, Philadelphia
www.morimotorestaurant.com
www.karimrashid.com
Karim Rashid
Project Team: Karim Rashid (Principal), Jalan Sahba (Space Director and Project Manager), Lisa Rusakova (Architect)
Client: Starr Restaurant Organization
Lighting: Focus Lighting, New York

Nectar, Las Vegas
www.mozer.com
www.bellagio.com/pages/din_nectar.asp
Jordan Mozer & Associates
Client: MGM Mirage

Nomads, Amsterdam
www.concrete.archined.nl
www.restaurantnomads.nl
Concrete Architectural Associates
Project team: Rob Wagemans, Gilian Schrofer, Erik van Dillen, Jochen de Blay, Esther Visser, Frouke Visscher, Onne Walsmit
Client: Bert van der Leden, IQ Creative

Oggi, Stuttgart
www.lamott.de
Lamott Architekten
Project team: Caterina Lamott, Prof Ansgar Lamott
Client: Maurizio Estrano, Romano Cardascia
Flooring/bar (stone): Fa. Fliesen Körner
Kitchen/bar equipment: Fa. HOGAKA
Panelling bar (wood)/furnishing/glass: Fa. Dillmann
Chairs: RIVA
Lighting: Spectral
Art: Sinje Dillenkofer

Opium, Sydney
www.misho.com.au
Misho + Associates
Project Team: Misho, Olga Gruzdeff, Jane Dillon, Fleur Kay, Anthony Bowden, Joe Hitti.
Client: Mr Wolfe Pizem
Sculptor: Horst Kichle of Amorphous Constructions
Foreman/Builder: Eric Giardullo of DFK Interiors
Structural Engineers: Nick Joanides, Partridge Partners
M&E: Donnelley Simpson Cleary
BCA Consultants: Trevor R. Howse and Associates
Acoustics Engineer: Louis Challis
Cardboard Sponsor: Visy
Structural Steel: Lee Tunks, 'Man of Steel'
Flooring Supplier: Second Hand Building Centre
Partitions/Ceilings: B+B Interiors
Mechanical Contractor: Sovereign Air
Plumbing: Plumbing Contractors of Paddington
Door Hardware: Metropolis Hardware
Joinery: Sterling Interiors
Excavations: Tip Talk
Sanitary Suppliers: Reece Plumbing
Tiling Supplier: Terracotta salvaged from Renzo Piano Building
New Tiles: Glennon Tiles, Tiler: Metz

Pearl, Miami Beach
www.dupouxdesign.com
www.penrods.com
Dupoux Design
Client: Jack Penrod
Staff Uniforms: Lubna Zawawi

Pod, Philadelphia
www.rockwellgroup.com
www.podrestaurant.citysearch.com
David Rockwell Group
Project Team: David Rockwell (Principal), Sam Trimble (Senior Associate-in-Charge), Jun Aizaki (Project Manager), Kimberly Silvia Hall (Senior Interior Designer), Yael Behar, Jennifer Morris
Client: Stephen Starr, Starr Restaurant Organization
Consultants: DAS Architects (Architect of Record)
Main Contractor: Domus
Lighting Consultant: Next Step Design Group
MEO Consultants: Steven R. Shore Consulting, C.J. Engineers, Inc.
Dining Chairs: Terminal-NYC
Lounge Table: Pure Design Studio
Lounge Ottomans: Totem UK
Concrete Flooring: Azzarone Contracting
Painted Wall Finish: Price Thomas Studios
Resin Bar Top: Atta Inc.
Silicon Tube Curtain: Sansei Builders

(Alain Ducasse at) Plaza Athénée, Paris
Patrick Jouin
Client: Plaza Athénée
Project Manager: Tania Cohen
Main Contractors: Poltrona Frau (leather seating)
Ets Roger (furniture, luster sideboard)

R, Paris
Christophe Pillet
Project Team: Christophe Pillet, Delphine Waiss (Project Manager)
Collaborators: SA Montal, Studio Architecture Bruno Huet (Architect on Site)
Client: SA MONTAL
Project Management: Norisko Construction, Cabinet S3C
Acoustics: Acoustique Pierre Poubeau
Groundworks: Sté des Rosettes
Woodwork: Sté AMCE
Paintwork: Sté E.B.R.
Heating and plumbing Engineer: Sté CIMO
Ventilation and Air conditioning: Sté ALIZE
Electrical Engineer: Sté ITE

Rumi, Miami
www.nancymahdesign.com
www.rumimiami.com
Interior Design, Lighting Design, Project Management: Scott Kester, Principal of Nancy Mah Design
Interior Finishes: Nancy Mah of Nancy Mah Design, Katy Colby
Project Team: Leonard Camposano, HeeSeung Lee
Architect of Record: STA Architectural Group
General Contractor: Terremark Construction
Furniture: J&P Decorators, Le Jeune Upholstery, Koss nc.
Flooring: Cozzolino
Custom Furniture and Lighting: Nancy Mah Design
Custom Tile: Hunnell Street Tile Works
Custom Brick: Ait Manos
Speciality Finishes: Industrias Exporenso Limitada
Custom Metal Balusters: Metal Heads, Inc.

Sketch, London
Design Concept: Mourad Mazouz, Noé Duchaufour-Lawrence
Client: Mourad Mazouz
Parlour Furniture: Jurgen Bey
Interior of The Lecture Room: Gabhan O'Keeffe
Interior of The Library Toilets: Mehbs Yaqub
Crystals in Bathrooms, Curtains in The Library and Lecture Room: Swarovski
Soup Trolleys: Marc Newson
Sculptures in Entrance Hall and West Bar: Vincent Leroy
Chandelier in East Bar: Marc Newson
Sculptural Desk in Lobby: Ron Arad
Invisible Sculpture on Stairs and Laser Lights in West bar: Chris Levine

Spoon Byblos, Saint-Tropez
www.byblos.com/spoonbyblos
Patrick Jouin
Project Manager: Tania Cohen
Client: Spoon Alain Ducasse
Main Contractors: Matinox (kitchen, technical furniture, inox furniture, Laval sideboard and all other furniture).

Supperclub Roma, Rome
www.concrete.archined.nl
Concrete Architectural Associates
Project Team: Rob Wagemans, Gilian Schrofer, Erik von Dillen, Onne Walsmit, Esther Visser, Pino Rocca.
Client: Bert van der Leden, IQ Creative

Tao, New York
(www.schoos.com)

Project Credits (continued)

Tangerine, Philadelphia
www.scheferdesign.com
David Schefer Design
Project Team: David and Eve-Lynn Schefer
Client: Stephen Starr, Starr Restaurant Organization
Lighting Design: Johnson Schwinghammer
Chairs: Munrod
Banquettes (wood): Spring & Down
Fabric: Pollack & Associates (banquettes), Designtex (banquettes), China Seas (banquettes), Osborne & Little (burned-out velvet draperies)
Leather: Dualoy
Plaster Ceiling Domes and Decorative Painting: Terra Firma
Drapery Fabrication: Maen Street
Bar Stools: See
Decorative Plaster: Visions in Plaster/Four Leaf
Decorative Lighting: Isaac Maxwell Metalworks
Carpet and Accessories: Gates of Morroco
Glass Bar Top: Galaxy Glass

Tuscan, New York
www.jeffreybeers.com
Jeffrey Beers International
Project Team: Jeffrey Beers (Principal), Michelle Biancardo, Jae Lee, Gil Rampy, Madeline Ruiz-Robinson, Lisa Sinclair, Martin Weiner
Client: Jeffrey Chodorow, China Grill Management, Inc.
Main Contractor: Bronx Builders
Tables: JC Furniture
Chairs, Ottomans, Bar Stools, Mezzanine Lounge Furniture: Erre Studio
Upholstery: Designtex, Glant, Cortina Leather, Holland and Sherry
Wenge Ceiling/flooring: Norwegian Floors
Art Glass Wall: Amanda Weil Studio
Wall covering: Designtex
Stone walls, Bars, Flooring, Veneto glass: Stone Source
Custom Draperies: Mary Bright
Fabric: Pollack Associates
Lighting: Steven McKay, Artemis
Wine Loft Cladding: Landmark Architectural Metal and Glass
Lighting Consultant: Johnson/Schwinghammer
Art Consultant: Museum Editions
Museum Editions: Millwork

WasabiSabi, Hong Kong
www.glamorous.co.jp
Original Concept: David Yeo
Design Theme/layout: Yasumichi Morita, David Yeo
Design Details: Yasumichi Morita, David Yeo, Satomi Hatanaka, Seiji Sakagami
Architectural Drawings and Project Liaison: Katsumi Ota
Graphics: Kenichi Inamoto, David Yeo
Client: David Yeo
Contractors: Plan-In Ltd
Lighting Consultant: Kenji Itoh
Sound System and Gobo Lighting: Sun Wong

Wildfire, Sydney
www.wildfiresydney.com
www.bucich.com
Bucich Studios
Client: Tonci Farac
Contractor/Builder: Arcon
Design Concept: Tonci Farac, Mark Miller
Graphic Design: Ronny Ruhlman
Furniture: Cabas
Cane Furniture: Antiga
Lighting: ECC Lighting
Kitchen and bar design: Tonci Farac, Mark Miller, Neils Danielsen of Wildfire Restaurant Concepts
Kitchen and Bar Fit Out: Austmont Catering

Yabani, Beirut
Bernhard Khoury Architects
Project Team: Bernhard Khoury (Project Architect), Fardi Sarieddine (Project Manager), Patrick Mezher, Michele Maria
Client: Bizen 1
Main Contractor: Fundamentals
Consultants: E.P.M.E.C, A.C.I.D
Graphic Design: Black Trombone

Author's Acknowledgements

At Laurence King Publishing I am most grateful to Commissioning Editor Philip Cooper for commissioning the book and to Jennifer Hudson for her patience and persistence in researching and gathering all the information, which eased the writing process considerably. To my editor, Liz Faber, your calm approach was invaluable, many thanks.

To all my contacts around the globe who have recommended projects for the book; in particular Roger Cave in Hong Kong, Mark Leib in Sydney and jetsetters Eric Yu and Angus Winchester – thanks for your roving eyes and reliably good taste. Vanessa and David Basto, thanks for putting me up on my New York research trip, and to my long-suffering partner Damon, thanks for putting up with me whilst I dragged you around Paris and New York.

Designers Giff and David Azurdia at Blast, you've been great to work with as always. Many thanks, especially for barely raising an eyebrow when I requested all those annoying, last minute changes. Rob Lawson, our ever-ready photographer, yet again you've done wonders. Thanks are also due to Modus PR for supplying the Alessi cutlery for book photography, and to Pam Carter and Nick Green for assisting in this area too.

And finally, a huge thanks to all the architecture and design practices, restaurateurs, press officers, photographic agents and photographers who have spared their precious time and provided me with the inspiration, information and material that has made this book possible. This is book is dedicated to you all.